THE
GIANT'S CAUSEWAY
AND THE NORTH ANTRIM COAST

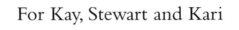

For Kay, Stewart and Kari

THE
GIANT'S CAUSEWAY
AND THE NORTH ANTRIM COAST

Philip S. Watson

THE O'BRIEN PRESS
DUBLIN

First published 2000 by The O'Brien Press Ltd.,
20 Victoria Road, Dublin 6, Ireland.
Tel: +353 1 4923333; Fax: +353 1 4922777
E-mail books@obrien.ie
Website www.obrien.ie
Originally published in 1992 by HMSO Belfast
and the Environment and Heritage Service,
Belfast, 33 Castle Street, BTI IGU.

ISBN: 0-86278-675-4

1 2 3 4 5 6 7 8 9 10
00 01 02 03 04 05 06 07

The O'Brien Press receives
assistance from

The Arts Council
An Chomhairle Ealaíon

Layout, editing, typesetting and design: The O'Brien Press Ltd.
Colour separations: C&A Print Services Ltd.
Printing: Zure S.A.

CONTENTS

ACKNOWLEDGEMENTS

Special thanks are due to the Environment and Heritage Service of the Department of the Environment for Northern Ireland for generous provision of illustrations, and for their help in general.

The author is grateful to numerous individuals and organisations for supplying information and advice over many years, in particular to the following: Robert Anderson, Ruth Blair, Tommy Cecil, Cahal Dallat, Hill Dick, Philip Doughty, Sammy Gault, John Greer, Mike Hartwell, Gary Hewitt, Frank Holden, David Hutchinson, Ian Irvine, Johnny Johnston, James Kane, Morris McCurdy, Tom McDonald, Liam McFaul, Neil McFaul, Kevin McGarry, Bertie McKay, Ross Millar, Sean Morton and David Speers; the Bushmills Folklore and History Group; the Department of Agriculture for Northern Ireland; the Department of Economic Development for Northern Ireland; the Department of the Environment for Northern Ireland, in particular the Environment and Heritage Service, including the staff of the Portrush Countryside Centre; The National Trust, Northern Ireland, and Cirencester, Gloucestershire, England; the North-East Education and Library Board (Irish Room, Coleraine); the Northern Ireland Tourist Board; the Public Record Office of Northern Ireland; the Ulster Folk and Transport Museum; the Ulster Museum; and the University of Ulster at Coleraine.

My thanks to all at The O'Brien Press Ltd in Dublin for their help and encouragement.

None of this work would have been possible without the continuing support of my wife, Kay.

PREFACE

This book evolved from an earlier one, published in 1992, which is now out of print.

Like William Thackeray – the Victorian novelist and author of *The Irish Sketch Book of 1842*, who took a boat trip to the famous stones – I had my first views of the Giant's Causeway and its spectacular coastline from a small boat on a heaving sea. Fisheries studies in the mid-1970s took me in and out of the Causeway bays, under magnificent headlands, in pursuit of lobster and crabs. A decade later, I began to explore the landscape on foot, during ecological and local history surveys.

As I have had the privilege of such close contact with the fishing and other local communities, and the plants and animals of the sea and land, it is not surprising that my perception of the Causeway coast is one of superb landscapes and seascapes, populated and visited by interesting people and supporting a wealth of wildlife.

For readers wishing to explore the geology in more depth, Paul Lyle's excellent *Geological Excursion Guide to the Causeway Coast*, published in 1996, is recommended. I therefore make no apology for emphasising the human and wildlife interests of the Giant's Causeway's story, at some expense to geology; others better qualified than myself in this discipline have already done an admirable job (see Bibliography). In these pages, the strange stones of the Causeway are part of an equally fascinating story of fishermen, farmers, seaweed-gatherers, smugglers, boatmen, guides, storytellers, artists, poets, writers, philosophers, naturalists, travellers, tourists and celebrities. All these have proved that the famous Dr Johnson was wrong when he answered Boswell's question, 'Is not the Giant's Causeway worth seeing?' with the words, 'Aye, worth seeing, but not worth going to see.'

Philip S. Watson
January 2000

MYTHS AND MISTS

Legends and Stories

WHERE THE NORTH COAST OF IRELAND FACES THE ATLANTIC OCEAN, WITH SCOTLAND VISIBLE TO THE NORTHEAST ON CLEAR DAYS AND NORTH AMERICA – SOMEWHAT FURTHER AWAY – OVER THE WESTERN HORIZON, A HUGE PAVEMENT OF SYMMETRICAL COLUMNS OF A DARK ROCK CALLED BASALT DESCENDS FROM THE BASE OF HIGH CLIFFS INTO THE WATER. DID A GIANT WITH A BUILDING BEE IN HIS BONNET CREATE THIS HONEYCOMB-LIKE CAUSEWAY, OR DID THIS MYSTERIOUS PLACE HAVE A NATURAL ORIGIN?

Each year, up to half a million visitors from all over the world ponder this question when they come to see the Giant's Causeway. The site is easily accessible; it is on the north coast of Co Antrim, about 100 kilometres (just over sixty miles) north of Belfast, Northern Ireland's capital city. The nearest town, three kilometres (two miles) from the Causeway, is Bushmills – a name known to all who appreciate Irish whiskey.

Myths arose before science, and the two meet at the Giant's Causeway. Long before UNESCO declared it Ireland's first World Heritage site in 1986, locals boasted that this strange arrangement of stones was a wonder of the world. In the old days – before there were geologists – the coastal folk stories of Co Antrim claimed that the Ulster hero Finn MacCool was the creator of the Giant's Causeway.

In the Finnian tales, Finn is described as the leader of the armies of the King of Ireland, Cormac mac Airt, in the third century AD. Finn the fighter, Finn the hunter with his favourite hound Bran, Finn of the knowledge gained from eating the magic salmon – a man of so many parts is easily mythologised. Finn

tore a sod of earth from mid-Ulster and hurled it at a rival in Britain. He missed, and the missile became the Isle of Man, in the middle of the Irish Sea; the hole left in Ulster filled with water and became Lough Neagh. His son, Ossian, a poet, and his grandson, Oscar, carried the tradition forward; but it is mainly Finn's name we remember, and it is a prefix in many Irish and Scottish place-names.

Generations of local guides, boatmen and souvenir-hawkers embroidered the tales of Finn, elevating him to the status of a giant – to the amusement (and occasional irritation) of their customers, the tourists.

The core of their legend goes something like this:

One of various 'giants' at the Causeway.

A Tale of Two Giants

Long ago, an Irish giant named Finn MacCool roamed the north coast, where he could look across the narrow sea of Moyle to Scotland. A Scottish giant, Benandonner, was Finn's greatest rival, challenging his strength and reputation. As the two giants had never met, Finn decided to invite Benandonner to Ireland, to engage in a decisive battle. There was no boat large enough to carry giants, so Finn built a causeway of huge stones across the water so that the Scottish giant could travel on dry land; thus he would have no excuse to avoid the confrontation.

However, as big Ben approached, Finn realised to his horror that his opponent was a larger and more fearsome rival than he had anticipated. He fled to his home in the nearby hills, and, like any sensible man, asked his wife for advice. Oonagh, a practical woman, disguised Finn as a baby, complete with large nightgown and bonnet. She placed him in a huge, hastily made cradle, telling him to keep quiet and pretend to sleep, as Benandonner's great shadow darkened the door.

Oonagh brought the Scottish giant in for tea, pleading with him not to waken Finn's child. Looking at the massive 'baby' lying in the cradle, Benandonner took fright, saying that if this was the child, he had no wish to meet the father. He fled back to Scotland, ripping up the Causeway behind him, terrified that the awful Finn might follow him home.

This, claims the legend, is why it is known as the Giant's Causeway. Those who remain sceptical are shown the open water, Scotland on the horizon, and a pile of broken Causeway columns, which mark the destructive haste of the fleeing giant.

The Irish may have a reputation for enjoying a fight, but trickery won the battle on this occasion.

Variations on this theme exist, and the story can be extended, with details of the 'child's' exploits. Some tell of Finn building the Causeway to bring home a wife from Scotland, or to visit a lady-love, a giantess. The Scottish giant is sometimes called Fingal, and this name is preserved in Fingal's Cave, the basalt columns on the island of Staffa that locals claim are the other end of Finn MacCool's famous Causeway.

To give credence to their tales, the Causeway guides of former years named various physical features in the bays and around the headlands after the giant. Stand on the Causeway and look west, across Port Ganny bay. On the landward side of the Stookans, the little hills at the far end, is the hunched profile of an old woman struggling up the hill. This is the Giant's Granny. She was climbing the hills to supervise Finn as he laboured at building the Causeway; when he could stand her nagging no longer, he turned her to stone. With some help from a modern guide, and a good deal of imagination – perhaps fed by a Bushmills whiskey or two – you might also find in the area the Giant's Harp, the Giant's Eyes, his Organ Pipes, his Chimneys, his Cannons, his Pulpit and more. It may

Artistic licence at the Organ.

The Giant's Harp – curved columns of basalt.

be helpful to refer to the walks recommended in Chapter Seven, with an occasional glance at the maps provided.

The Measure of a Giant

Some will argue that a mythical giant lives best in our minds, and needs no illustration or other evidence. But children (and adults) visiting the Causeway often ask how big Finn MacCool might have been. For the pub-quiz fanatic, the definitive answer is sixteen metres (fifty-two feet and six inches). The clue which leads us to this colossal statistic is the Giant's Boot – a large rock, weathered to the shape of a boot, which lies on the shore in Port Noffer, about 200 metres from the east face of the Causeway. The author – may he be forgiven – took detailed measurements of the Giant's Boot and submitted this evidence, together with photographs, to a number of institutions and scientists. They entered into the spirit of the inquiry, although eventually all but one admitted defeat. The answer came from a forensic anthropologist in South Carolina, who supplied a formula based on her research into ancient footprints. From this came the measure of Finn. So, indeed, myth and science meet at the Giant's Causeway!

Causeway Folklore

The stories told by guides over the past three centuries sprang largely from their own imagination and wit, with the giant at their core. There is a rich collection of folklore and stories in the Glens of Antrim, east of the Causeway coast; Cahal Dallat's book *Antrim Coast and Glens: A Personal View* (1990) will give readers a feeling for this. Rathlin Island, lying a few miles off Ballycastle, also has a rich folk history. The folklore of the Causeway is inevitably mixed with traditional beliefs, tales of giants and historical events from the time of the Vikings and earlier.

Some stories are associated with place-names. There is a local belief that Vikings camped, beneath their upturned longboat, at the Brenther harbour in the bay below the Giant's Causeway Centre; the name 'Brenther' is derived from Old Norse words meaning 'steep harbour'.

A more reliable link with Norsemen is found a little way along the coast, at Dunseverick Castle. The Annals of Ulster record that Vikings raided the castle twice, in AD870 and AD924; the nearby jagged promontory of Benadanir – 'the peak of the Danes' – is a reminder. Also at Dunseverick, a legend tells how Conal Cearnac, of the Red Branch Knights of Ulster, was present at Christ's crucifixion in Jerusalem, where he subsequently helped push aside the boulder from the mouth of the cave of the resurrection. Another story records how Turlough O'Cahan of Dunseverick returned from the Crusades to find the fortified promontory of his home occupied by the Danes, and his sister forcibly engaged to their leader, Hakon Jarl. Turlough disapproved, and in the ensuing battle both men were killed and the site was burned. The grief-stricken girl leapt to her death from the cliff. Thereafter, it is said, the banshee of the

The Giant's Boot.

O'Cahans, Granie Roe, could be heard wailing over the roar of the sea in winter storms. (Banshees are female spirits, usually attached to specific families; they are, according to tradition, most noisy around the time of a death.)

The Causeway does not hold a monopoly on giants. The imposing cliffs of Fair Head, near Ballycastle, are 194 metres (636 feet) high, and are composed of huge columns of dolerite, a hard volcanic rock; they are the home of another giant, known as the Grey Man. He has been seen by fishermen in the area, in the shape of a grey-cloaked giant rising from mists swirling over the water and about the headland, in the vicinity of the chasm known as the Grey Man's Path. In 1858 the Grey Man appeared near the Causeway, at the mouth of the River Bush, again, he was a tall, grey-cloaked figure, standing on a pillar of a bridge in a wild flood.

Fairies feature strongly in stories from the Glens of Antrim, but one Causeway tale in particular is worth mentioning. In *Rowlock Rhymes and Songs of Exile* (1933), a book of north Antrim poems in Ulster Scots, there is a tale recorded as 'The Piper and the Fairies'. According to this tale, a local piper by the name of McKibbin was dozing on a Causeway headland after drinking his profits at the end of a Causeway Fair. He was kidnapped by the fairies and taken to a nearby cave, where he remains to this day. McKibbin was also condemned to play the tune 'The Farther in the Deeper' for a hundred years.

A daring pose at the Grey Man's Path.

For over 300 years, since the Giant's Causeway first became an object of public interest, visitors have been subjected to tall tales as well as to more traditional folk stories. Gradually science crept in, as naturalists, philosophers and geologists debated the natural origin of these unusual rocks. Guides responded to their more serious patrons, who wanted some solid information, and began to slip in a bit of geology – while never letting the facts ruin a good story. Giants, perhaps, earned them larger tips than geology.

The guide performed his office satisfactorily and most obligingly but it would be an improvement if guides could be brought to describe natural appearances correctly and omit the senseless jargon about Giants.

This dry comment was written on 7 April 1876, by the President of the Geological Society of Glasgow, in the logbook of Causeway guide John MacLaughlin. John had netted a serious academic in his daily trawl of customers. Others, in search of entertainment, were more appreciative of his wit and blarney, which were proffered readily, if at a price:

We the undersigned sojourners in this land whose air is fatal to small silver placed ourselves in the hands of our guide the genial John MacLaughlin and found him an honor in his Profession and cheerfully recommend him to all Travelers. Signed, Henry Miller and Chas. H. Edgar of New York and H.A. Potter of Philadelphia, July 1877.

A REMNANT OF CHAOS

Geology and Scientists

MON DIEU! *AND HAVE I TRAVELLED A HUNDRED AND FIFTY MILES TO SEE* THAT?

On a stormy autumn day in 1842, William Thackeray, rigid with fear and clutching the seat of a small boat, had his first glimpse of the Giant's Causeway, and was not impressed. Later, safely ashore and contemplating the strange rocks in more detail, he allowed himself to speculate:

When the world was moulded and fashioned out of formless chaos, this must have been the bit *over – a remnant of chaos!*

William Makepeace Thackeray was in his early thirties when he came to Ireland in 1842 – a decade or so before his major novels (*Vanity Fair*, *The Virginians* and so on) were published – to write a travel book. Like many visitors', Thackeray's first impression of the Causeway from a distance was a disappointing one. As with Finn MacCool's first sight of his great rival Benandonner, the reputation of the Giant's Causeway is only confirmed at close quarters. Then the question forms in your mind: 'If not made by giants, then how?'

William Thackeray visits the Causeway, 1842.

In the eighteenth century, naturalists, philosophers and scientists argued this question at length as they pondered the origin of basalts. It was the 1820s before the volcanic theory was accepted (see Chapter Three).

But a fiery birth does not explain all the features of the offspring. Why such precision? Why so many six-sided columns? What made the domes and hollows of their surfaces? And when did all this happen?

The True Story of the Giant's Causeway

Lava cools and becomes rock. At the Causeway, this is a fine-grained hard rock called basalt.

The immediate impression is one of amazing regularity; the whole Causeway looks man-made. The individual columns – remnants of a deep lava-flow – are mainly five- or six-sided; they are so tightly packed that they form a pavement-like structure. The causeways – there are three promontories – extend into the sea but do not, despite the legends, continue underwater to Scotland; the strange stone formations cease quite abruptly, and the seabed offshore is largely composed of sand, shell and gravel. Large, angular boulders between the causeways are the fractured remains of hard intruded dykes, where later lava flows forced their way to the surface through weaknesses in the ground.

The natural origin of the Giant's Causeway, which was formed about 60 million years ago, is generally understood to have occurred as follows:

Imagine lava at 1,100°C – eleven times hotter than boiling water – hissing and sparking its way into a hollow, which was probably once a river valley. The lava begins to cool, losing heat to the rocks below and the air above. Cracks zigzag across the surfaces, shattering the shiny new rock to give a honeycomb effect. As the cooling and shrinking progresses through the depth of this volcanic pond, columns are formed. These cool throughout their length, and stresses cause curved cross-cracks, splitting the columns into amazingly equal-sized tablets of stone, each one fitting on the next like a ball-and-socket joint. The result is a geometrical layout of rocks, like a huge, uneven patio. Domes and hollows are obvious features on the top of the Causeway, and the shallow depressions in the tops of the columns nearest the sea are often glittering with salt crystals where little pools of sea water have evaporated.

If the cooling process had been perfectly even, all the columns would have six sides, like the cells of a honeycomb – an efficient way to fill a space. But cooling varied, influenced by seeping fresh water, and amongst the 40,000 or so columns of the Giant's Causeway are some with four, five, seven, eight or even

'The Chimneys' at Port na Spaniagh.

nine sides. You may be lucky and find the only three-sided stone.

What makes the Causeway special is the fact that it offers a chance to see this wonderful jointing, in both the vertical and the horizontal plane, so easily. This is rare: it is more usual to find columns of basalt partly exposed in cliff-faces – as can be seen within the World Heritage Site at locations such as the Organ, the Amphitheatre and especially Plaiskin Head, all of which are visible from the Causeway and Dunseverick Castle walks described in Chapter Seven (see maps). A spectacular display of columns in a cliff and cave exists at Fingal's Cave on the Scottish island of Staffa, which lies off Mull, a little over 100 kilometres (sixty miles) over the sea to the north of the Causeway.

Visitors often ask if the Causeway was made by hot lava cooling suddenly in the sea, or if it grew like crystals. Although crystals do occur in parts of the Causeway coast lava flows, in former gas bubbles, the Causeway columns are not themselves crystals. Neither are they the product of lava sizzling and spluttering into the sea. Between 60 and 55 million years ago, when the Causeway lava was flowing, the sea level was much lower, thus the lava cooled in the air, or on existing cool rocks. If it had poured into the sea, features such as pillow lavas would be found.

Local people are very proud of the Giant's Causeway; early guides were inclined to boast that no such thing existed anywhere else in the world. Scientists, unfortunately, often explode myths, and they have discovered columns of basalt similar to the Causeway in many countries. Few, however, are as much visited, wondered at and mythologised as these stepping stones curving gently towards Scotland from Ireland's Atlantic north coast.

The volcanic features are not restricted to the Causeway itself. Three major layers of basalt make up a sandwich-cake of geology along the Causeway coast cliffs, with the icing between the layers represented by red and brown laterite (from the Latin *later*, a brick), which contains iron and bauxite ores. Further east, near Port Moon, and inland, these ores were mined to produce iron and aluminium, the peak extractions being in the 1870s.

Opposite the Giant's Causeway, looking east towards the isolated pillars known as the Chimneys, up to seven lava flows can be identified. The lower basalts are distinct here: about five dark bands in the cliffs, from sea level up to a broad streak of red laterite. This colourful layer separates the lower basalts from the middle basalts, which contain the spectacular columns and similar structures, such as the nearby distinctive arrangement of pillars known as the Organ. Further inland, there is another deep band of reddish inter-basaltic soils, on top of which sit the upper basalts, which are non-columnar. Along the coast further to the west, these stretch down to sea level; but erosion over a long period has removed them from the Causeway area.

Former lava flows in cliffs opposite the Causeway.

This arch collapsed in the 1940s.

The many layers of lava flows – some with perfect columns, some with starchy, twisted, cruder columns, some of irregular shape – together with the red, brown, purple and grey inter-basaltic bands, can be viewed along the cliff-top path from major headlands such as Plaiskin, Benbane and Bengore. The bays, headlands and promontories from Portnaboe to Benbane Head show classic features of the geology of the Tertiary period, which lasted from about 65 million to around 2 million years ago. This was a volcanic time in the Earth's history, and the superb legacies of that violent time, which have survived in the Causeway landscape, are rightly recognised by the World Heritage Convention.

The coastline we see today has been shaped by millions of years of weathering under near-tropical conditions; by ice ages, the most recent of which ended between 20,000 and 10,000 years ago; and by the attacks of the sea when, due to melted ice sheets, the ocean level was much higher than it is today. The relentless wear and tear of rain and wind and frost also helped to sculpt the coast and continues to affect its rocks and soils. All these conditions produced the great curved bays, leaving narrow necks and headlands where the sea still takes bites out of the land. In addition to volcanic features such as extruded lava flows and intruded dykes, the landscape includes raised boulder beaches, rock platforms, islets and sea stacks – some the remains of collapsed arches. All these provide clues to landscape formation, and are reminders that this remains a dynamic coastline.

Even if you are not interested in geology, you cannot fail to be impressed by the colours and the rugged beauty of the Causeway's surroundings.

FROM BISHOPS TO BIOLOGISTS
Discovery and Descriptions

IN 1692, THE BISHOP OF DERRY AND AN UNNAMED CAMBRIDGE GRADUATE VISITED THE GIANT'S CAUSEWAY. TRAVEL IN IRELAND WAS DIFFICULT IN THOSE DAYS, AND ACCOMMODATION WAS SCARCE AND OF POOR QUALITY. THE BISHOP AND HIS COMPANION WERE CREDITED WITH THE 'DISCOVERY' OF THE GIANT'S CAUSEWAY FOLLOWING A LETTER PUBLISHED IN THE *PHILOSOPHICAL TRANSACTIONS OF THE ROYAL SOCIETY* IN 1693; THE LETTER WAS WRITTEN BY SIR RICHARD BULKELEY OF CO WICKLOW, WHO HAD OBTAINED A DESCRIPTION FROM THE CAMBRIDGE SCHOLAR.

The Causeway stones must have been known to local residents, many of whom fished, gathered seaweed and grazed stock in the area, but the 1693 letter is the first known publication describing the Causeway. It was not marked on a map until 1714.

Between 1692 and 1708, a number of eminent clerics, scholars and naturalists commented on the newly discovered Giant's Causeway. Dr Samuel Foley, Bishop of Down and Connor, who contributed his views on the Causeway to the Royal Society in 1694, also included the first known image of the phenomenon, an engraving by Christopher Cole. Sir Thomas Molyneux, originally from Castle Dillon in Armagh, visited the Giant's Causeway on a journey north from Dublin in 1708. In 1717 he became Professor of Medicine at Trinity College Dublin, and did much to advance learning in Ireland, for his interests included geology, archaeology and history. He wrote a detailed description of the Causeway, and arranged for a sketch of the site to be made by Edward Sandys in 1696.

Molyneux was the first to discuss the basaltic nature of the rocks, and he was not shy about dismissing the stories of giants. He claimed that those with no knowledge of natural history were usually inclined, when they did not understand the origins of unusual natural phenomena, to name these after giants, fairies, demons and suchlike. His views are to some extent borne out by the number of columnar rock structures around the world with such references, eg, 'The Devil's Postpile' (California), 'The Devil's Tower' (Wyoming), 'Fingal's Cave' (Scotland – Fingal the giant) and 'The Adamantine Gates of Hell' (Tasmania).

After the first decade of the 1700s, little more was heard of the site until the middle of that century. The story of the Causeway leapt into the headlines once again, in a manner of speaking, with the production, in 1740, of several spectacular paintings of the east and west prospects of the site. These were by a little-known Dublin artist, Susanna Drury, who received a prize of twenty-five pounds for her work. What little is known about her is summarised by Martyn Anglesea and John Preston in their detailed account of her Causeway paintings' relationship to the known geology of the time, published in the journal *Art History* (September 1980) as 'A Philosophical Landscape: Susanna Drury and the Giant's Causeway'. We have to admire the determination of this middle-class Dublin lady in travelling to this remote site to sit by a rugged shore to paint! In 1743-1744, François Vivarès produced detailed engravings of Drury's two main views, and the circulation of these around Europe revived interest in the Giant's Causeway. The illustrations contained enough detail to enable scientists and others to form theories about the formation of such rocks.

Neptune versus Vulcan

This heavyweight fight in the late 1700s was conducted for the sake of knowledge and of scientific honours. Scientists are as capable of passionate argument as any other human beings. Throughout the eighteenth century, the science of geology was undergoing upheavals, as debates on the origins of the Earth's rocks heated up. Igneous rocks, such as granites and basalts, featured in these controversies, which ran almost as hot as the Causeway lava.

Scientists studying the origins of basalts and similar rocks fell into two camps. Those supporting the theory of fiery origins were labelled Vulcanists, while those who believed in marine sediments as the source were known as Neptunists. Thanks to the Drury/Vivarès illustrations, the Giant's Causeway was known to these learned men.

A view of the headlands from Hamilton's Seat.

In the Vulcanists' corner, the main contenders were Nicholas Desmarest of France (1725-1815) and James Hutton (1726-1797), a famous Scottish geologist. Leading the Neptunist contingent were Abraham Werner (1749-1817), a charismatic and influential German teacher of geology, and one R. Kirwan from Ireland, who, in the 1790s, brought the debate to the local scene on the Causeway coast: he claimed to have discovered marine fossils in basalt at Portrush in Co Antrim, near the Giant's Causeway. These fossils are embedded in layers of an ancient shale, 150 million years older than the lava which baked these sediments hard. Kirwan's case, published in 1799, was soon disproved. By the 1820s, the theories of the Vulcanists were generally accepted, and the origin of the Giant's Causeway was no longer seriously disputed.

The Portrush rock (not the sweet type with letters all the way through!) is now a National Nature Reserve, and is well worth a visit. It is on the shore by Ramore Head car park, facing Portrush's East Strand. The nearby Portrush Countryside Centre provides a wealth of information on the natural and local history of the Causeway coast, including these famous debates.

Absent from these arguments were the views of another local man, the Reverend Doctor William Hamilton, a keen naturalist and rector of a nearby Co Donegal parish, who spent the summer of 1784 exploring the Causeway headlands, sometimes on horseback. Hamilton's letters on the natural history of basalt were first published in 1786. He correctly interpreted the Causeway and its surroundings as volcanic in origin, and his writings were the first to relate the Causeway to accurate descriptions of the surrounding landscape. Hamilton's Seat, opposite Plaiskin Head, which was one of the Reverend Doctor's favourite spots, is named in his memory. Sadly, he was murdered near Lough Swilly in Donegal in 1797, in the unrest preceding the rebellion of 1798.

Geologists continued to take a great interest in this coastline, and the mid-twentieth century saw significant developments in the study of basalts. In 1940, the Russian-born geologist Sergei Ivanovich Tomkieff developed a new way of describing the main features of the Causeway. In an interesting alternative view to the Romantic movement's earlier fascination with nature as architecture, he saw in the levels of columnar basalt flows a parallel with classical Greek temple architecture. The lower, regular columns of a typical Causeway flow he called the colonnade; the less regular layer above he dubbed the entablature. This is exemplified in the Organ, where the tall columns resemble the colonnade (or pillars) of a temple, supporting the entablature (the blocks laid across the top) – in this case, the tightly packed, rather prismatic rock above the Organ.

The Romantics

The Reverend Hamilton referred to the Causeway coast scenery as 'natural architecture'. He lived at the beginning of the Romantic movement, which saw links between art and nature. In the Georgian periods, visitors to the Causeway were seeking a renewal of the human spirit and a chance to immerse themselves in romantic landscapes. Such places were described in language that depicted columns, cliffs and caves as Gothic cathedrals and palaces. Engravings from this period exaggerated the cliff scenery of the area and took artistic licence with the number and size of the Causeway columns. This led to some visitors being disappointed with the reality, as we shall see later.

Poets, too, were attracted by this romantic view of nature and visited the Causeway at this time. Sir Walter Scott, arriving in 1814, was feeling unwell and not inclined to lavish descriptions – unlike W.H. Drummond, who, in the following extract from his epic 1811 Causeway poem, appears to have a partial understanding of the Vulcanists' views:

Did plastic nature in the flood of flame
Each hexagon, concave and convex frame?
Then, did refrigeration's gelid power
Freeze the dense column, pyramid and tower?

Appreciation of the sublime seems to have been high on visitors' agendas throughout this period, when nature, art and the human response to both of these were in vogue. Edmund Burke, who in 1757 wrote of the sublime as 'a sort of tranquility tinged with terror', saw in the oceans' various moods an expression of this human need for a response to wildness in nature. The Causeway landscape obviously fulfilled this need. In 1845, one Richard Lowry from the north of England, taking a boat trip at the Causeway, recorded in his diary:

... floating upon the bosom of the mighty Atlantic – the sight was certainly grand ... At no other spot can the sublime scenery be seen with so much effect.

Guidebooks and Travel Writers

In 1788 one of the first popular guidebooks, entitled *The Complete Irish Traveller in the Kingdom of Ireland*, was published in two volumes. This contained a good description of the Giant's Causeway.

Guidebooks proliferated during the 1830s and 1840s, by which time almost all travellers in Ireland had the Causeway on their itinerary. Regular features about the famous stones appeared in popular magazines of the nineteenth century, such as the *Dublin Penny Journal* and the *Illustrated London News*.

Naturalists, many travelling in field club excursions, were anxious to see the Giant's Causeway and air their new-found knowledge, gleaned from the rising tide of geological papers that included references to the Causeway. Photography, too, was contributing to interest in the site; prints were published in the 1860s, and by the 1880s and 1890s these photographs were appearing regularly in guidebooks, alongside the more traditional engravings and sketches.

People and Nature

The rugged terrain around the Causeway has little evidence of early human settlement. In the grasslands and scrub set back a short distance from the coast, however, archaeologists have identified some burial sites, former settlements, hiding places, ritual sites and standing stones, spanning almost 7,000 years, from around 5,000BC (the transition from the Middle to the New Stone Age) to the arrival of the Anglo-Normans in the twelfth century. For example, there are Stone Age tombs, which required some degree of co-operation to build, at White Park Bay and along the ridges just inland of Ballintoy. There are many other ancient sites in the area, dating from periods ranging from the Bronze Age

The Belfast Naturalists' Field Club at the Causeway, 11 June 1868.

Fossils of ammonites in Lias shale at Portrush.

(around 2,500BC) to the time of the Vikings' arrival (the ninth and tenth centuries AD). For example, there are two fine double-ringed earthworks at Lisanduff, above Portballintrae car park; and a number of circular earthworks or raths are scattered along the coastal hinterland. Souterrains (man-made underground passages lined with stone, used for storage and as hiding places) are also found in the area – at Aird, near the Causeway, for example, and at Dunluce Castle. Add to these the occasional standing stones, promontory forts (for example, at Larrybane, near Carrick-a-Rede) and a few caches of buried Viking ornaments and coins, and the north coast has its fair share of what local archaeologist Jon Marshall has referred to as 'forgotten places'.

Since the 'discovery' of the Giant's Causeway over 300 years ago, geologists have tramped the ground regularly. In general, biologists and naturalists have been less in evidence. There are some interesting nineteenth-century references to plants and birds, but it was the eminent Irish naturalist Robert Lloyd Praeger who recognised the area's overall natural richness. In his autobiographical *The Way That I Went* (1937), he sang the praises of the Antrim coast's geology, archaeology and botany, and noted that the remains of the extinct great auk – a huge, flightless seabird – had been excavated from the Neolithic settlement in White Park Bay.

The photographer R.J. Welch (1859–1936) was another fan of the Antrim coast, and he recorded many geological and landscape scenes. He was also an enthusiastic student of land snails, and Murlough Bay and Fair Head were among his favourite hunting grounds.

The first biological surveys of the Giant's Causeway area were carried out in 1985 and 1992, by teams of field surveyors from the National Trust, and in 1991 a team from Lancaster University took a close look at the plant communities of the cliffs and bays. Marine surveys of Northern Ireland's inshore seabed were conducted over the years 1982–1985, and of the inter-tidal areas in 1984–1988; these provided valuable information on the Causeway coast's marine environment.

The shale and lava beds at Portrush, which featured in eighteenth-century geological debates.

Survey of the Causeway Coast's vegetation.

Thanks to these surveys, and to the work of individual biologists and local groups, the Causeway coast and adjacent shore and coastal waters are known to house well over 200 species of flowering plants, many seaweeds and marine invertebrates, over 100 species of birds, and at least eleven land mammals (excluding bats). Atlantic grey and common seals are both found, and at least ten types of whale, dolphin and porpoise have been identified. Over a dozen species of butterfly regularly occur – the grayling, red admiral, common blue, meadow brown and ringlet are worth looking out for – and the list of moths is growing. These figures are approximate, and are steadily growing as more biologists and naturalists explore the area. Most of us are unlikely to see such unusually named Causeway specialities as the pin-head squirt (a sea creature) and the narrow-mouthed whorl snail; but there is a slight chance of spotting, along the cliff-tops, one local rarity – the bilberry bumblebee, its plump body distinctively marked with a russet band at the rear.

MAKING A LIVING
Local Life and Natural Resources

PEOPLE HAVE BEEN COMING TO THE CAUSEWAY COAST FOR A LONG TIME. EXCAVATIONS AT A MESOLITHIC SITE AT MOUNT SANDEL ON THE RIVER BANN, JUST UPSTREAM FROM COLERAINE, SHOWED THAT A SETTLEMENT EXISTED THERE ABOUT 9,000 YEARS AGO. IN ADDITION TO GATHERING FOOD FROM THE NEARBY WOODLANDS AND FROM THE RIVER, THE INHABITANTS MADE EXPEDITIONS TO THE COAST TO CATCH FISH IN THE RIVER ESTUARY AND PERHAPS TO GATHER SHELLFISH ALONG THE SHORELINE. ABOUT 5,000 YEARS AGO, NEOLITHIC DUNE-DWELLERS AROUND THE COAST ALSO GATHERED SHELLFISH AND CAUGHT BIRDS. THE RELIANCE ON COLONIES OF SEABIRDS AND THEIR EGGS AS SOURCES OF FOOD WAS COMMON TO ISLAND COMMUNITIES OFF NORTHWEST SCOTLAND AND AROUND THE IRISH COAST, FROM RATHLIN AT THE EASTERN END OF THE CAUSEWAY COAST TO THE BLASKETS OFF CO KERRY. THESE ACTIVITIES ONLY CEASED WITHIN LIVING MEMORY; AS RECENTLY AS THE 1940s, GULLS' EGGS WERE HARVESTED AT RATHLIN.

There were risks in exploiting the natural resources of the sea, whether by venturing out in small boats to fish, by collecting seabirds and their eggs from cliffs and rock stacks, or by gathering seaweed at the foot of towering headlands. Even those in larger ships were not always safe, as lists of known shipwrecks around this north coast testify.

Fisheries

Along this exposed coast, men have rowed, sailed and chugged to sea in small boats for over 350 years in pursuit of fish, and salmon continue to be netted at sites known since 1630. The 1825 *Steamboat Companion to the Western Islands and Highlands of Scotland* reported that fishing boats from Portnahaven on the island of Islay were travelling the thirty miles to the Giant's Causeway to fish for cod, ling and turbot. As recently as 1926, the small harbours nearest to the Causeway – Portballintrae and Dunseverick – sheltered twenty working boats supporting fifty-four fishermen, including those who worked part-time. Due to declines in fish stocks, increased freight charges and alternative employment ashore, there are few full-time fishermen making a living today.

As well as fixing salmon nets at various shore stations, fishermen caught lobster, edible crab, buckies (whelks), cod, haddock, skate, ling, plaice and other fish living on or near the seabed. Fish nearer the surface, such as herring and mackerel, were also taken. In the 1920s and 30s, fishermen set long lines – some a mile in length – using hooks baited with mussels, limpets, salted mackerel or buckies. This method exploited fish stocks throughout the year, with hard days at sea in pursuit of winter cod.

The north Antrim fishermen worked in traditional boats, long lining for fish and potting for crab, lobster and buckies. Some had the advantage of an inboard engine for powering the boat, but others rowed or sailed. Without navigational instruments, the fishermen relied on long-established sight-lines to landmarks ashore to locate fishing grounds. Out of Dunseverick, for example, if a fisherman lined up the Carrick-a-Rede bridge with the north side of Sheep Island, the Causeway Stookans past the Chimneys and the Dunseverick Stookan, he would have been on a good ridge for cod. The fishermen's knowledge of the sea, and of the creatures they sought, was remarkable.

The sketch of Thackeray at sea off the Causeway in 1842, in his *Irish Sketch Book*, is notable in that it records very accurately the traditional boat of the north Irish coast at this time – a double-ended *drontheim*, otherwise known as a Norway yawl. These seaworthy vessels survived as fishing-boats well into the twentieth century, and they were a common sight in small coves and harbours around the Donegal and Antrim coasts, as well as on the Scottish island of Islay. There is a revival of interest in *drontheims* at present, and the risk that this unique vessel will become extinct has lessened.

Left: Finn MacCool features in ancient Irish tales as a Celtic warrior, but generations of storytellers at the Causeway saw him as larger than life.

Previous page: The soft light at sunset reddens the details of the Causeway's columns. The cross-fracturing of individual columns — split apart as they cooled from lava to rock — was curved, giving rise to convex and concave surfaces.

Below: The fort of Sobhairce occupied a strategic cliff-top promontory, reputedly once the capital of the Kingdom of Dalriada, where today the gaunt remains of an Elizabethan tower and walls survive, battered by Atlantic winds.

Above: Benandir ('the Peak of the Danes'), a jagged basalt promontory at Port Moon, close to Dunseverick Castle. Vikings raided this area in the ninth and tenth centuries. On this central part of the Causeway Coast, the cliffs gradually drop from a height of over 100 metres (300 feet) to sea level.

Below: From deep in the earth's crust, hot magma — at over 1,000 °C — fed the lava flows. When these cooled, they formed the basalt bones of much of the Causeway Coast's landscape.

Above: *There are roughly 40,000 columns, closely packed, in the Giant's Causeway. Guides often told visitors there were 39,996; when asked how they could be so precise, they would say that there had been 40,000, but a rich visitor had bought four and taken them away!*

Below: *Although most Causeway stones have six sides, there are four-, five-, seven- and even eight-sided exceptions.*

Above: Many lava flows created the layered landscape around the Causeway cliffs. The splashes of rusty red soils give a clue to their origin; long-ago weathering processes formed ores of iron and aluminium.

Below: Deep, shady bays and sharp headlands are characteristic of the Causeway World Heritage Site.

Above: Susanna Drury's mid-eighteenth-century paintings may have exaggerated the Causeway columns somewhat; nevertheless, they were the first reasonably accurate images, and they created great excitement among geologists of the time.

Right: Local guides of the eighteenth and nineteenth centuries gave names to many features — including the pipe-like columns of the Organ — to enhance their stories of the giant who, they claimed, had created the Causeway and the surrounding landscape.

Above: *Flowering gorse (whin or furze) adds to the colourful views along the cliff-tops in spring.*

Fishermen in earlier days near the Giant's Causeway.

The pursuit of salmon around the Irish coast has a long history. Bag nets, which took over from fixed draft nets in the 1830s to 1850s, can still be seen in summer at Port Moon and Carrick-a-Rede, and at other sites along the coast from Portstewart to Carnlough. Salmon, however, have become more scarce, and these nets are less numerous now.

Fishing has always been a hazardous way of life. Only great knowledge of the sea, and a healthy respect for it, minimised the risks. When the crews of the *drontheims* were working the salmon nets and fishing crabs, the fishermen often transferred their catches to passing fishing-smacks bound for Liverpool. These larger vessels were in such a hurry to return to port with their valuable cargoes that the transfers were made while the smacks were under sail. This sometimes led to tragedies, and crew members were lost when the smaller boats capsized.

Despite the hardships of the deep, humour was never far from surfacing. Consider the Dunseverick advice on seasickness: 'Take a large spoonful of jam before you go to sea – it won't cure the seasickness, but sure it tastes as good coming up as it did going down!'

The Cliff-Climbers

Today, almost a quarter of a million seabirds inhabit the cliffs, rock stacks, coves, caves and surging waters of Rathlin Island. Over a hundred years ago, Victorian naturalists viewed these busy breeding colonies with awe, referring to the 'whirring multitudes' of birds. The islanders had a more pragmatic approach: the birds, and their eggs, provided food over the short nesting season from May to August.

Climbing unaided up sea stacks, descending a cliff on a hemp rope or nosing

Cliff-climbing bird-hunters of Rathlin Island, with ropes, an egg-box, a gun and two freshly killed guillemots.

a small boat into a narrow cave and landing on a ledge, the bird-men ducked the roar of wings as panicking birds whizzed past, and took a harvest of eggs and birds to supplement their larders. Despite their remarkable climbing skills and detailed local knowledge, accidents happened; and inevitably, on such huge cliffs, there were fatalities. But in those days, fish and seabirds were important sources of protein, and cash crops were few.

One of these – also provided by the sea – was the annual kelp harvest.

The Story of Kelp

The cold, clear waters of the Atlantic Ocean and North Channel, and their rocky and cliff-bound shores, are ideal for the growth of the large brown seaweeds collectively known as kelp. In spring and summer, thick-stemmed oarweeds and other brown algae grow vigorously in these coastal waters; their wet brown stems and fronds can be seen glinting on the surface at low tide, or

Seaweed (wrack) at low tide in Portnaboe.

waving underwater – like a forest of trees in a gale – as the high tide swirls and pushes around them.

In winter, this rich growth dies off and storms loosen the kelp's hold on the rocks. Large numbers of stems and tangles of weed are washed ashore in coves, bays and beaches along the Causeway coast. In May, the 'cuckoo storms' throw up the last piles of this marine detritus, which is known locally as the 'May fleece'.

Today, these banks of seaweed are left to rot, picked over by birds in search of insects, shellfish and other marine creatures caught up in the tangles. However, from at least the eighteenth century to the 1930s, kelp was an important resource for northern and western coastal communities of Scotland and Ireland.

In the Causeway bays, the seaweed was gathered by hand, and the heavy, wet loads were carried in wicker creels, or on long-handled forks, to be piled to dry on low dry-stone walls specially constructed close to the tide-mark. Remains of kelp walls can be seen in Portnaboe and other bays to the east as far as Ballintoy. When the weed had dried, usually by June or July, it was laid on iron bars or similar grids over stone-lined pits, or kelp kilns, and burned. The molten residue, like a bluish sticky toffee, eventually cooled and hardened, and this product was also called kelp. It was bagged and, in the remoter bays, carried to the cliff-top to be collected by agents.

In a letter dated 13 August 1784, the Reverend Doctor William Hamilton records the fate of one particular kelp-gatherer called Adam Morning, who lived close to the Causeway.

One morning [in the summer of 1783] *as Adam and his wife were descending down the dangerous path to pursue their daily toil, while they were yet talking of their growing hopes, even while the cheerful prospect was smiling in their view, a sudden slip tumbled him headlong from the precipice and dashed him to pieces on the rocks below.*

Despite the risks of the work, kelp-gathering provided an important source of income to the farming and fishing families of the Causeway coast, and on Rathlin it paid the islanders' rents. The salts of sodium and potassium which came from kelp were essential in bleaching processes and in making soap and glass. The later discovery that iodine was present in kelp proved useful in medicine and photography, two applications which prolonged the industry through the late nineteenth century.

By the 1930s, modern methods of recovering large amounts of these chemicals from other sources destroyed the demand for kelp, and even the more recent exploitation of seaweeds for the alginate industry has not revived interest in the Causeway coast's marine algae.

The whitish smoke of kelp fires is no longer seen, but once it was a regular feature in summer on these northern shores. While it was probably an irritant to the kelp-burners, the pungent smoke was believed by some to have decongestant qualities. There are records that sufferers were prepared to take a lungful or two to alleviate bronchial troubles – perhaps the only case where smoking might have been good for your health!

Shipwrecks, Scavengers and Smugglers

Beachcombing, especially in the event of shipwrecks, has long been an established activity along the rugged Causeway coast. Many ships have come to grief along this north coast; Rathlin has about sixty known wrecks in the dangerous waters around the island.

In 1588, the wreck of the Spanish Armada ship *Girona* provided James McDonnell of Dunluce Castle with the opportunity to scavenge cannons and treasure, the latter probably in the form of coins and jewels from the bodies washed ashore. On 20 October 1869, travel writer Edwin Waugh was staying at the Causeway Hotel, which overlooks Blackrock and Bushfoot Strand. The liner *Cambria* was wrecked that night at the rocky islands of Inishtrahull, off the northern tip of the Inishowen peninsula opposite. Waugh noticed the wreck-gatherers; in his book *Rambles and Revelries*, published in 1874, he wrote:

... as I went towards the strand, I met cart after cart returning from the sea, laden with wreck.

Left:
The white smoke of kelp fires is a thing of the past.

The George A. Hopley, *an American square-rigger, wrecked off Portstewart in 1856.*

Over the years, timber, liquor, cloth, china and many other commodities found their way into local households. During the two World Wars, convoys attacked by submarines added to the list of tragedies, and often poignant personal effects of the sailors' would be washed up on these beaches.

The coastguards at Portballintrae – here pictured just over 100 years ago – were armed and kept busy in pursuit of smugglers. Edwin Waugh, mentioned above, enjoyed a chat with these men in their 'breezy man-o'-war garb', and was shown

A coastguard at Portballintrae, 1898.

'the arms of the station all sharp and bright and ready for action'. The coastguards' vigilance was particularly sharp in the narrow North Channel, which separates the Co Antrim coast from the Mull of Kintyre by as little as eleven miles. The Campbeltown Customs Records for the years 1739-1816 show that variations in excise duties and other taxes led to smuggling of horses, wool, salt, soap, hides, tea, tobacco and whiskies, both Scotch and Irish.

Jimmy Irvine, writing about the above records in 1976, described the scene:

... the coastlines on North and East Antrim and Kintyre seemed to have been specially designed by nature to assist the smuggler ... the crossing could be made in two or three hours in small open or half decked boats. These would pull up to load and land their secret cargoes in the many lonely creeks and coves with which these shores abound.

In 1812, barley was smuggled from Portballintrae to Islay for the manufacture of whiskey. By 1815, illegal whiskey distillation at Inishowen (north Donegal) had been stopped, and Islay whiskey was fetching double the price per gallon when smuggled the thirty miles to the north Antrim coast.

Mr Cross, the coastguard, Portballintrae, 1898.

Fairs and Regattas

Coast and country folk made their own entertainment, combining business with pleasure – as at a country fair where trade was shared with sports – or just getting together to pit their special skills against one another, as at regattas and horse races.

Many country fairs have disappeared over the past 150 years, but some survive. The Lammas Fair of Ballycastle, usually held over two days in the last week of August (although the traditional day of the Irish summer festival of Lammas is the first of August), dates from at least 1606. There was a Causeway Fair in the nineteenth century, and it was revived for a while in later years; it was held in summer in fields by the Causeway Head, with sports and entertainments such as tug-o'-war and pipers. Not all such diversions were in summer. The Bushmills Annual Horse Races were held in January each year on Bushfoot Strand; the first of these Races, in 1877, attracted around 10,000 spectators from townlands around the neighbouring parishes.

With the availability of the skills and strength of men making a living from the sea, it is not surprising to find that sailing and rowing regattas were also popular annual events. Summer regattas were held at most of the north- and east-coast ports,

Yellow Man – a sticky toffee – for sale at the Old Lammas Fair in Ballycastle.

from Moville in Donegal to Carnlough in Antrim. Traditional boats, such as *drontheims* and specially built rowing skiffs for crews of two or four oarsmen, were raced. One famous skiff, the *Arrow* of Port Moon, was celebrated by local poets; their verses, backed up by newspaper reports of the time, provide a record of the vessel's successes. James McAllister of Tonduff, near the Causeway, born in 1865, was probably referring to a regatta in the 1880s when he wrote:

> *The course being selected lay near Ramore Hill*
> *Where the boys from Port Moon met the men from Moville*
> *In their fast racing drontheim called Arrow by name*
> *Her crew and her coxswain – five heroes of fame …*

The Moville men had a priest along, to bless them as 'kings of the waves', but the crew of the *Arrow* beat them nevertheless! In 1985, the *Arrow* was rescued from decay in the Port Moon fishery bothy, restored and put on display in the Causeway Centre for a number of years. This unique vessel is in storage again, awaiting a suitable venue at her home of 'Lochaber shore' (the old name for the Causeway headlands), where she can be put on permanent display.

Causeway-like columns at an inland quarry near Ballintoy.

Mining and Quarrying

Not all commercial activities were sea- and shore-based. Iron and aluminium ores, present in the red soils between lava flows, were mined where these beds were thickest. The mines were spread around the Antrim basalt plateau, from north of Belfast through the Glens of Antrim to the north coast. The peak extractions took place from 1870 to 1880, although some mines continued to operate until the 1920s, and there were examples of old aluminium ore mines being re-opened during the Second World War.

A description of iron mining in Co Antrim was recorded by J. Hodges in his 1875 Presidential Address to the Belfast Natural History and Philosophical Society. He referred to the availability of local labour:

… a very short time was sufficient to convert the ordinary farm labourers of the district into excellent miners, able to pick from two to three tons of ore daily.

At this time, a miner with a little experience earned 15 to 20 shillings weekly.

There was a strong link between mining and quarrying and the development of railways, and tracks for mineral extraction were laid inland to formerly secluded glens, to facilitate transport of ores to shipping ports. The famous Giant's Causeway tram (described later) was conceived as a mineral railway, although it turned out to be a vital link for tourists between the main Portrush–Belfast railway line and the Giant's Causeway.

There were iron and bauxite (aluminium ore) mines along the Causeway coast. Most were driven horizontally into the red bed between the lower and middle basalts, a little way inland; but one was at the coast in Port Fad, just north of Port Moon, on the Causeway headlands. The ore at this site was run on buggies down a small track to a flat point halfway down to the sea, where it was tipped down a chute to small coasters waiting at a rather perilous berth below. It probably joined the ores from east Antrim mines, which were shipped to processing plants in Britain.

The coastal landscape is pitted here and there with the scars of basalt and chalk quarries, but few are active now. Columns of basalt were cut from exposures near Portrush and Ballintoy, and even the Giant's Causeway was not immune to such exploitation, as we shall see later. Many walls, farm outhouses and gate pillars along this coast, if examined closely, show the distinctive Causeway-type stones, which also served the builders of the ancient church of Templastragh, above Port Braddan.

Farming

Before the Second World War, farming in this coastal area coexisted with fishing, kelp-making, mining and quarrying. All these other activities have either died out or declined, and, as subsidies became available, farming intensified in the post-war years.

Much bogland and heath along the north Antrim coast has been converted to pasture, and considerable areas of rough grazing have been improved by the addition of fertilisers to boost grass growth and increase stocking rates of sheep and cattle. Coastal heaths and maritime grasslands, once rich in wild flowers and small birds, have been fragmented, and only patches survive near the cliff edges.

However, it has been recognised that traditional farming practices have helped to create attractive landscapes and valuable wildlife habitats in Northern Ireland. The designation of Environmentally Sensitive Areas by the Department of Agriculture for Northern Ireland has encouraged farmers to join these voluntary schemes. The Department provides advice and financial incentives to participating farmers, to help them protect and enhance the conservation value of their land. Along the Causeway coast, work within these schemes has, for example, preserved traditional gate pillars, repaired dry stone walls, improved hedgerows and encouraged heather regeneration, and there is a special programme of aid to protect the feeding habitat of one of Northern Ireland's rarest birds, the red-billed crow called the chough.

Diversification has led to some other farm-based activities, such as providing bed and breakfast, fishing ponds, pony trekking and even the occasional small golf course. Farming continues to be a dominant influence on this coastal landscape, providing a patchwork of small fields and clustered settlements or *clacháns*, which are attracting the attention of developers of holiday homes.

Spanish Treasure

The traditional story that a Spanish Armada ship sank near the Giant's Causeway in 1588 was preserved in local place-names: Port na Spaniagh, Spaniard Rock, Spanish Cave and the Spanish Organ. Numerous nineteenth-century guidebooks and other published accounts of the area, as well as tales told by local guides up to the mid-twentieth century, described how the ill-fated ship foundered in a storm under the rock pinnacles known as the Chimneys. Some claimed the ship had fired her cannons at these rocks, mistaking them for castle turrets, but this seems an unlikely act for the crew of a ship within minutes of disaster.

Why, then, with all these local clues, was it almost 400 years before the Belgian salvage diver Robert Stenuit and his team discovered the few remains and rich contents of this ship at Port na Spaniagh and proved it to be the galleass *Girona*? In *Treasures of the Armada*, his account of the *Girona* find, Stenuit points out that historical records were inaccurate, tempting divers to search further to the west, in the area between the mouth of the River Bush and Dunluce Castle.

In 1967, on a preliminary visit along the cliff path to Port na Spaniagh, Stenuit and a companion read, in a guidebook they had bought at the Giant's Causeway, how the galleass *Girona* was wrecked at a little cove near the Giant's Causeway, still called Port na Spaniagh. Nobody took the local folklore seriously; but after extensive research, Stenuit – amused to find his theory confirmed in a cheap pamphlet – decided to dive in Port na Spaniagh. On June 27 1967, during his first dive in thirty feet of water at the east face of Lacada

Point, he saw a white shape. It was a lead ingot.

Arching my back, I heaved it over, and there stamped on the upper face were five Jerusalem crosses. I had found the wreck.

Nearby, during the same dive, he discovered an Armada cannon, cannonballs and other artefacts. Over the summer diving seasons of 1967, 1968 and 1969, Stenuit and his helpers brought out of Port na Spaniagh a fabulous treasure of gold and silver coins, gold chains, personal jewellery and decorations of the ship's officers and crew, including the Knight of Malta cross belonging to Don Fabricio Spinola, the captain of the *Girona*. These treasures, and other artefacts recovered from the *Girona* and the *Trinidad Valencera* – another Armada shipwreck, discovered by divers of the Derry Sub-aqua Club in 1971 – are preserved in the Ulster Museum at Belfast, where some are on permanent display. The folklore was right, after all.

Today, the towering columns and jagged rocks of Port na Spaniagh are as awe-inspiring – indeed terrifying – as they must have seemed to the 1,300 or so sailors, soldiers and noblemen who struggled and drowned in this bay on the night of 26 October 1588. There were few survivors; accounts list between five and thirteen, whom James McDonnell of Dunluce helped to return to Spain.

The Reluctant Tourist

I believe that you will be astonished at seeing this letter on account of the slight certainty that could have existed as to my being alive ...

Thus begins an extraordinary first-hand account of a survivor of one of the Spanish Armada ships wrecked off Ireland in the autumn storms of 1588. Captain Francisco de Cuellar was transferred from his ship, the *San Pedro*, to another, one of three wrecked at Streedagh Strand in Co Sligo. Surviving great hardships, Captain de Cuellar spent over three months in the northwest of Ireland, eventually making his way on foot to the vicinity of Dunluce Castle, near the Giant's Causeway (unknown at that time).

... at the end of twenty-one days' journey, I got to the place where Alonzo de Leyva ... with many other gentlemen, were lost ...

CAPTAIN CUELLAR'S

ADVENTURES

IN

CONNACHT & ULSTER

A.D. 1588.

A PICTURE OF THE TIMES, DRAWN FROM CONTEMPORARY SOURCES.

By HUGH ALLINGHAM, M.R.I.A.,

Member of the Royal Society of Antiquaries (Ireland);
Author of "Ballyshannon: its History and Antiquities," &c.

TO WHICH IS ADDED

An Introduction and Complete Translation

OF

CAPTAIN CUELLAR'S

Narrative of the Spanish Armada

AND HIS ADVENTURES IN IRELAND.

By ROBERT CRAWFORD, M.A., M.R.I.A., &c.

With Map and Illustrations.

LONDON : ELLIOT STOCK, 62, PATERNOSTER ROW.
1897.

A Spanish Armada survivor's story from 1588.

He was told by locals:

… of the great misfortunes of our people who were drowned at that place, and [they] showed me many jewels and valuables of theirs, which distressed me greatly.

De Cuellar managed to find help, and was shipped to Scotland and from there collected by a ship from Flanders. He was shipwrecked again off Dunkirk, but survived and eventually reached sanctuary in Spanish-controlled Antwerp, from where he wrote his account in a letter to a friend. This was not published until 1885, in Madrid, as part of a work entitled *La Armada Invinciple* by Captain Caesaro Fernandez Duro, a Spanish naval officer. The narrative 'Captain Cuellar's Adventures in Connacht and Ulster, A.D. 1588' is thrilling reading, and is a rare account of northwest Ireland at the time of Queen Elizabeth I's rule in Britain. Perhaps de Cuellar was the first tourist – albeit a reluctant one – at the Giant's Causeway!

BOATMEN, GUIDES AND ENTERTAINERS
Hosts and Tourists

THIS CHAPTER BEGINS IN THE 1790s, IN THE FINAL PHASE OF THE MORE RELAXED ROMANTIC MOVEMENT'S INTEREST IN THE CAUSEWAY, MOVES ON TO THE 1840s, AND TRACES THE RISE OF MASS TOURISM IN THE SECOND HALF OF THE NINETEENTH CENTURY. LOCAL PEOPLE LIVING AROUND THE CAUSEWAY, MANY OF WHOSE FAMILIES WORKED AS BOATMEN AND GUIDES, CLAIM THAT IN THE NINETEENTH CENTURY THROUGH TO THE YEARS BETWEEN THE TWO WORLD WARS, THE SITE WAS AS BUSY AS IT IS TODAY.

Visitors to the Giant's Causeway in the latter part of the eighteenth century, like tourists today, had three main requirements: accommodation, transport and the expectation of seeing something authentic, even unique. The ingenuity of local people met these needs and expectations with the provision of inns and hotels; transport in horse-drawn wagons, traps and small boats; the invention of the

Right: Sailing to the Causeway in 1900.
Left: A souvenir-seller at the Causeway's Wishing Chair in the late nineteenth century.

world's first hydroelectric tram; and the use of their natural wit and persuasion to enhance the visitors' experience of seeing the Giant's Causeway. Another motive was at work: to relieve the tourists of their cash.

Donal McCracken, reviewing the Georgian periods at the Causeway, wrote in the *Journal of the Glens of Antrim Historical Society* in 1985:

Notables were able to inflict themselves on the local gentry, but ordinary travellers were faced with a considerable problem. The two great hotels at the Causeway were products of the middle nineteenth century. Portrush was a little fishing village where in 1752 no lodgings were to be found.

Prior to 1806, there was no decent accommodation at Bushmills, the nearest village to the Causeway. McCracken concluded that the Georgian visitors:

... were never in number and mostly from the upper strata of society ... The Causeway was the preserve of the scientist, naturalist and romantic.

But all this was to change. Travellers in Ireland at this time began to write accounts of their adventures, and the travel book proliferated. As the number of visitors grew, guidebooks appeared in profusion – and, of course, with these came guides.

Wanderers such as the French emigrant Le Chevalier de la Tocnaye in 1796, and visitors from nearer areas, such as the Reverend Dr William Hamilton of Donegal in 1783-1784, often moved about on horseback. Both wrote lively accounts of their visits to the Causeway, the former in romantic terms and the latter with the sharp observational powers of the amateur naturalist. Anne Plumtree of Cambridge wrote of two summers' residence in Ireland, in 1814 and 1815. She took a guide from Ballintoy – about seven miles east of the Causeway – and walked to the famous site along the cliff-tops. Near Hamilton's Seat, she was intercepted by the Causeway guides:

... these men are like a parcel of hungry eagles, always hovering about, watching for prey, and the moment any is espied, the contest is commenced which can first pounce upon it.

William Thackeray expressed his own views about the boatmen-guides who, during his 1842 visit, bundled him into a boat much against his better judgement:

400/87 Portcoon Cave, Giant's Causeway

Boat trips into Portcoon Cave were once popular at the Causeway. The man on shore, with a bucket and long net, collected his tips after firing a gun to generate echoes around the cave.

... for after all, it must be remembered it is pleasure we come for — that we are not obliged to take these boats. Well, well! I paid ten shillings for mine, and ten minutes before would cheerfully have paid five pounds to be allowed to quit it.

Another English visitor — Mrs Hall, touring Ireland with her husband in 1840 — had a more kindly view of the guides they encountered at popular sites. Mrs Hall says that the guides in Wicklow and Kerry '... delight in legends of fays and fairies, and they greet you with a jest and bid you farewell with a tear'. She described the northern guides at the Causeway as follows:

... of the earth — earthy; of the stone — stoney; they have the mystified look of philosophers, and the youngest and most ragged has a certain affection of learning that is very amusing. They are, however, attentive and obliging.

Who were these guides? Where did they live, and how did they operate?

John McConaghy, who in the 1960s was the National Trust's first warden at the Giant's Causeway, recorded his memories on audio tape in the 1950s:

I don't think now there are any boatmen, or combined boatmen-guides, at the Giant's Causeway. But in the old days — and I'm referring to the period before and after the First

World War — there were dozens of them, and each man was a real character in his own right.

The guides lived in the various townlands and villages along the Causeway coast, and made a living from their activities during the tourist season. Boatmen were able to combine this with a bit of fishing, but the guides had to reap what they could in summer from the tourists. Edwin Waugh quoted a local woman's view of guiding in 1869:

The life o' a guide is a scattered thing … in summer it's a' chops, an' steaks, an' mutton, an' tay, an' whiskey, an' when winter comes … sleepin' an' shiverin' till the time gaes roun'.

Throughout the nineteenth century, a range of guidebooks to Ireland was available, and descriptions of facilities at the Giant's Causeway give a good idea of how accommodation and services had improved since the Georgian times.

During the 1830s, the Causeway Hotel, run by a Miss Henry, was established as an inn. Here, Thackeray, still uncomfortable from his boat ride, found sanctuary from the guides and had dinner and a good wine by a bright fire.

Baddeley's guidebook of 1887 lists the Causeway Hotel tariffs for boat trips with guides. Visitors were charged four shillings for 'the short course' and six shillings for 'the long course' (Thackeray was robbed when he was charged ten shillings almost fifty years earlier). The short trip included excursions into one or more of the nearby caves, then a voyage across the bay to the Causeway. The longer voyage also took in the superb scenery of the bays and headlands further east.

One 'entertainment' laid on to impress and amuse the boatloads of visitors took place at Portcoon Cave. Once inside, a boatman would give a signal, and an assistant — who had earlier been landed on a ledge at the mouth of the cave — would discharge a gun so that the clients could enjoy the echoes throughout the cave. The passengers' reactions varied, depending on whether or not they had been forewarned of this event. To receive his share of the takings, the gunner would reach out a long-handled fine net as the boats left the cave, at the same time hoping that the boatmen would remember him at the end of the day — for it was not unknown that he would be forgotten, left to languish on his cold perch while his colleagues drank their takings in the comfort of a hotel.

Much the same array of schemes and scams to relieve tourists of their cash existed at Killarney as at the Causeway, as is recorded on an annotated nineteenth-century postcard published by William Lawrence of Dublin:

Alec McLernon (guide) and Mary Kane (water-provider) at the Wishing Well, Giant's Causeway, before the First World War.

Taste the mountain dew [probably whiskey or poteen], hear the wondrous echoes, buy bog oak and arbutus ornaments, and purchase photographs.

At the Causeway, as well as being offered the Portcoon experience, tourists were exposed to a hard sell on various specimens of minerals from the basalts, small representations of the Causeway carved from the stones, photographic albums of local scenes and, to accompany their drink of water from the Giant's Wishing Well, tots of Irish whiskey. A succession of elderly ladies worked their patch by a small spring at the Little Causeway, offering a cup of water and a wish to tourists. Some supplied whiskey, and some, of a more 'good-living' background, frowned on this practice and would not. Thackeray remarked of the whiskey-seller at the Causeway:

She has no change for a shilling: she never has; but her whiskey is good.

The specimens mentioned above included fossils. Although the Causeway rocks are volcanic and do not contain fossils, this was no deterrent to the initiative of the guides. They collected fossils at places such as White Park Bay and Kinbane Head, and, when demand outstripped supply, imported them from Devon. In winter, the guides were able to replenish their fossil stocks, but not without risk. Two guides were drowned off Ballintoy in 1894, during a boat trip to collect fossils at Kinbane Head, despite heroic efforts by coastguards and local fishermen to try and save them; the three other occupants of their boat were rescued.

In Esler's guidebook of 1884, there is the story in song of 'Little Irish Nell', who proffered specimens for sale at the Causeway. The song was written for a Miss Nelly Hayes, who performed it on stage:

> Who'll buy a box of specimens just gathered from the strand?
> I've Irish diamonds fit to deck the proudest in the land;
> With amethysts and jaspers too, that sparkle in the light,
> And gems that glance like ladies' eyes, with lustre rare and bright.
> The price is only half-a-crown, I really wish to sell;
> Do buy a box of specimens from Little Irish Nell.

The boatmen took advantage of their captive audience to sell boxes of specimens. At some point in the journey, the oars would be shipped, and a box, wrapped in many layers of paper and bound with lots of string, was produced. The unwrapping took enough time for the sales pitch to reach full eloquence, and the customers perhaps had a feeling that a failure to purchase would delay their progress to the Causeway even further. Thackeray described this particular sales technique with some vehemence:

> The boatmen insist upon you looking at boxes of 'specimens', which you must buy off them; they laugh as you grow paler and paler, they offer you more and more 'specimens'; even the lad who pulls number three, and is not allowed by his comrades to speak, puts in his oar, and hands you over a piece of Irish diamond ... and scorns you.

Boat trips were popular at the Causeway through to the inter-war years, as were excursions to and from the stones by pony and trap, up and down the road known as the 'quality rodden' (probably referring to the 'quality' people as patrons, rather than to the condition of the road, which was often in poor repair). But in the 1880s, a new invention added to the modes of transport available for getting visitors to the site.

An artistic impression of the Causeway Tram passing Dunluce Castle.

The Causeway Tram

Child to Minister: *Did God make the tram?*
Minister: *Of course He did. Sure, didn't He make all creeping things!*

From 1887 to 1949, the Causeway tram creaked its way along the spectacular coastal route from Portrush to a terminus by the Causeway Hotel. Conceived and built by a local engineer, Dr William Traill, the tram drew its power from turbines at a mill on the River Bush, close to Bushmills. When it began running in 1883 (at this point it ran only to Bushmills; it was extended towards the Causeway four years later), it was the world's first commercially operated hydroelectric tram.

The tram became very popular with visitors and locals, although Traill had first intended it for transporting minerals. The railway from Belfast had reached Portrush in 1855, and a link was needed to the Causeway. For many years, horse-drawn carriages had ferried passengers to and from the Causeway; now there was a new and exciting form of transport.

In 1887, the tram carried 64,000 passengers. Its arrival in the grounds of the Causeway Hotel – which had the benefit of electric lighting from the same system – enabled the guides attached to this hotel to gain exclusive access to the passengers. Kane's Royal Hotel nearby, built in 1863, was in competition with the Causeway Hotel, and attracted a number of guides who operated as 'outsiders' – freelancers of a sort. This advertisement was displayed locally by the Royal Hotel in 1890:

As the tram is in connection with the Causeway Hotel, and arrives in its grounds, the ROYAL HOTEL is looked upon as opposition, and is not allowed a Porter to represent it at the Tram Depot. A Porter from the Royal Arms Hotel, however, attends on the Public Road, which is the nearest way to the Giant's Causeway. Pay attention to his call; don't mind the Tram Touters.

The 'Royal' prefix came from a visit by the Prince of Wales, later to become Edward VII, who was given a cup of tea; he granted permission for the new title.

At first, the Causeway tram drew its power from an electric rail which ran alongside the tracks at a low level. There was a certain naïveté about electricity in these early days, and William Traill, to demonstrate the rail's apparent safety to an inspector, dropped his trousers and sat on it. Only some time later did he admit to having received several painful shocks. The power line was later shifted to overhead wires.

During the Second World War, American servicemen arrived in Northern Ireland, providing welcome additional custom for the tram, which by then was beginning to suffer competition from motor cars. These soldiers, sailors and

The saloon and toast-rack carriages of the Causeway Tram at the Causeway Hotel terminus, around 1900.

airmen spent their money on trips to see the Causeway; but they were the last boost to business, and the decision to close the tram was made at the end of 1949.

Today, there are few relics of the tram left. Stumps of the power poles survive along the road by Dunluce Castle, and two carriages, a saloon car and a partially open 'toast-rack' carriage, are preserved in the Ulster Folk and Transport Museum. The tram lives on in local memories, and its character has been caught in this extract from tram-enthusiast Brian McAlister's lament:

> *Out beyond the White Rocks,*
> *Scootin' from Portrush,*
> *Headin' for the Causeway,*
> *Headin' for the Bush;*
> *Watchin' from the Toast-rack*
> *The hedge slippin' by,*
> *Dizzy on the cliff-top-*
> *Ye felt that high.*
> *Scatterin' the seagulls*
> *Round about Dunluce*
> *Paddlin' through the fields again*
> *Just like any goose;*
> *Left behind by motor car,*
> *Charabanc and bus,*
> *Though ye whizzed an' clanged along,*
> *Ratin' twenty plus.*

The route of the Causeway tram – between Bushmills and Causeway Head, alongside the River Bush and across the Bushfoot sand dunes – is to become a small railway, adding to the tourist attractions of the area.

Americans at the Causeway

The logbooks kept by guides in the nineteenth century were signed by many visitors, who endorsed their individual guide's qualities and possibly added some humorous comments or a few lines of verse. Records from two surviving logbooks, covering the 1860s and 1870s, show numerous entries by Americans hailing from New York across to California, although the eastern and central states and cities predominate. Visitors from New York, Boston, Philadelphia,

Cincinnati and Chicago (and many from Canada, too) enjoyed the wit and company of Causeway guides such as John MacLaughlin and James Hutchinson, and many others. Resident expatriates praised the Causeway, and no doubt their recommendations added to the flow of American visitors:

Christmas 1869. Edw. D. Neill, Consul, U.S. of America at Dublin, found the guide an intelligent expounder of the geologic structure of the peculiar finger work of God, called the Giant's Causeway.

The quarrying of Causeway stones for sale to tourists (discussed later in this book) led to many rather heavy souvenirs finding their way to the United States. A complete cluster of pillars was once extracted, shipped and re-erected in a public park in Philadelphia.

The Giant's Causeway Centre hosts visitors from all over the world, with up to fifty nationalities being recorded in any one year. The presence of many American signatures is evidence that the tradition of signing a book has lasted over a hundred years, even if the wit and wisdom of local guides have gone (although there are moves in hand to establish new guiding services at the Causeway).

CARING FOR THE CAUSEWAY
From Exploitation to Conservation

T HE CONCEPTS OF PROTECTION AND CONSERVATION CAME TO
THE GIANT'S CAUSEWAY IN 1961, WHEN THE NATIONAL TRUST
ACQUIRED THE SITE. BUT TO UNDERSTAND THE NEED FOR THIS, IT IS
NECESSARY TO RETRACE THE CAUSEWAY'S HISTORY, SELECTING
RELEVANT EVENTS FROM THE EIGHTEENTH AND NINETEENTH
CENTURIES.

Blood from the Stones
Stephen Gwynn, in *Highways and Byways of Donegal and Antrim* (published in
1899), described how he arrived at the Causeway in 1898 to find it:

*... tourist-ridden with a vengeance. Besides, a company has enclosed it with a railing, and
makes visitors pay sixpence for admission – an innovation started Easter Monday of this
year, which every good Irishman resents.*

Changes in ownership of the Giant's Causeway, plus its increasing popularity as
a tourist destination through the nineteenth century, contributed to the almost
inevitable development of commercial exploitation. The Causeway and
surrounding lands belonged to the Earls of Antrim from at least 1734, but were
leased to a John McCollum, becoming a permanent fee-farm grant in 1738. In
1796 the site passed, through marriage, to the Lecky family. There was, however,
confusion over details of the leasing arrangements, and the Antrim family
disputed points of ownership for many years. This led to demonstrations of
authority: Lord Antrim erected pillars, and the Leckys removed them; in the
1840s, the Leckys permitted Causeway columns to be taken for building; in
1863, they erected a caretaker's house on the very edge of the Grand Causeway.

Access to the Giant's Causeway was fenced off (close to the house) from about 1898 to about 1961.

The damage caused by these activities came on top of years of local quarrying of the stones for sale as curios and souvenirs, as remembered by John McConaghy in the 1950s (who, a decade later, found himself charged with the Causeway's protection when he was employed by the National Trust):

I'd like to mention the fact that in my days, the boxing of Giant's Causeway pillars was quite an industry. The guides and boatmen used to quarry these pillars and box them and send them off to Australia and Canada and the United States of America.

By the end of the nineteenth century, the Causeway was receiving an estimated 80,000 visitors each year, and in 1896 the Leckys leased it to a syndicate called the Giant's Causeway Company, which declared its intention of enclosing the site and charging admission. After two hundred years of free public access, this understandably caused considerable protest. A committee to defend the Causeway was formed, and in March 1897, the case came to court in Dublin.

This was – and is – an interesting case in Irish Property Law, and the defendants challenging the Lecky ownership contended that there were public rights of way to and over the Causeway stones, and that there were local customary rights to enjoy the various features of the site.

Every piece of evidence to support the defendants' case was sought. Maps, and even reproductions of the Drury prints, the Vivarès engravings and older illustrations, were produced to support the long history of public interest and use, and to show that paths existed to the Causeway. Guides and other locals were cross-examined in court. However, the judge found that there was no declared intention to create public rights of way, nor was there a proven right to wander at will over the site. The Leckys' right to ownership was upheld, and the Giant's Causeway Company was therefore able to pursue its intentions. An appeal followed, but also failed; and on April 16 1898 – Easter Monday – the new arrangements for admission and charging commenced, under the administration of the syndicate.

Enclosure did not diminish the tourist numbers. The first motor car arrived at the Causeway in 1910, and the site remained a popular place to visit throughout the First World War. The 1920s and 1930s – the inter-war years – were a 'golden age' at the Giant's Causeway; this feeling is still strong in living memory among the local communities. At this time, both large hotels were flourishing, guides and boatmen were in full swing, tramloads of visitors arrived regularly and the small shops and tearooms along the Causeway bays did a strong, if seasonal, trade. A travelling community, arriving at Easter and leaving at the end of September, provided visitors with additional entertainments, from fortune-telling to harmonica-playing.

During the Second World War, the Royal Hotel remained open, while troops were billeted at the Causeway Hotel; but soon this strongly commercialised age began to wane, and by the 1950s there were few guides left. Another change was in the air.

Early motor cars at the Causeway Hotel.

End of an Era

In 1961, the Giant's Causeway was transferred from private to public ownership, and the emphasis began to shift from commercialisation to conservation.

In 1960, the National Trust, a voluntary organisation dedicated to the preservation of places of historic interest or natural beauty, secured an option to purchase the assets of the Giant's Causeway Company, as well as the freehold interests of the Lecky family. Lord Antrim, chairman of the National Trust's Committee in Northern Ireland at this time, continued his family's interest in the Giant's Causeway: he encouraged the necessary purchases, in 1961 and 1962, which brought the Causeway, and surrounding bays and headlands, into the public ownership of an organisation with the right to declare its properties inalienable – in other words, they cannot be sold except by parliamentary consent. This is a powerful and long-term way of holding sites for the benefit of present and future generations.

The Trust set about tidying up the approaches to the Causeway. The turnstile and railings were pulled out, admission charges ceased, and gradually all of the surviving shops and other buildings were removed (some retained their business in kiosks at a site behind the cliff-tops at Causeway Head). The Trust established its own tearoom and a small information point, but never intended to remove visitor services entirely. It was thought desirable, and in keeping with an effort to return the Causeway's immediate environment to as natural a condition as possible, to move these services to a less intrusive location.

Not unnaturally, there was some resentment of this on the part of former Causeway traders, who felt that all these conservation ideals harmed their ability to continue to make their living. New opportunities for employment arose, however: the Trust took on local staff to repair and extend footpaths and to serve the public in the tearoom and information building, and they appointed their first warden in 1967.

Fresh Air and Exercise

The spectacular coastline which spreads out to the east and west of the Giant's Causeway was increasingly realised to be a great natural asset, offering opportunities for superb walks. But natural erosion of the cliffs and slopes had created dangerous gaps and overhangs; together with the changeable Atlantic weather, high cliffs and local landowners' concerns about people crossing their land, this made public access quite a challenge. It was also important to avoid disturbing plants, birds and other wildlife.

As boat trips had ceased, there was an urgent need to improve the coastal paths. In 1964, following purchases, covenants and other agreements between the National Trust and local landowners, sixteen kilometres (ten miles) of cliff-top path from Runkerry to Dunseverick Castle were declared open to the public. Between 1968 and 1978, various work schemes supported by employment agencies enabled the Trust to improve this coastal path network, including the breathtaking lower cliff path from the Causeway to Hamilton's Seat. In 1977 and 1978, surveys were carried out to locate bird breeding sites and to examine ways of minimising disturbance to wildlife in general.

What the Visitors Want
In 1980, the Northern Ireland Tourist Board carried out a major survey of the visitors to the Giant's Causeway. The 'Troubles' in Northern Ireland had certainly affected tourist numbers in the province, and there was a real fear of making the effort to come to the Six Counties – a fear that was proving difficult to overcome for those promoting a region where positive aspects such as the beauties of the countryside and the friendliness of the people were undermined by alarming news headlines.

Throughout the Troubles, the Giant's Causeway remained a strong attraction to visitors who had made the effort, and the famous stones became, more than ever, an icon which the tourism industry used to sell Northern Ireland as a destination in these difficult times. The north Antrim coast, while not escaping terrorism completely, offered a haven for the day tripper as well as for the tourist. Journalists and other media representatives from all over the world, in the province to cover stories on the Troubles, almost always took a trip to see the Causeway; and therein lay wonderful opportunities to communicate – for free – the better side of life in Northern Ireland – opportunities that were well-utilised right up to and after the 1994 IRA ceasefire.

The 1980 survey showed that visitors were, on the whole, reasonably satisfied with the Giant's Causeway. But, when asked what they might like to see in a visitor centre if one were provided, they showed a strong preference for legends, folklore and crafts, geology and the *Girona*. There was also an interest in finding out more about the local flora and fauna.

New Partnerships
In the 1980s, although the National Trust owned the Giant's Causeway and many other natural and historic sites along the north coast, the land at the

cliff-top approach to Causeway Head was owned by another public body – the local government authority, currently known as Moyle District Council.

The Council, with some responsibilities for tourism, made the decision to build a major visitor centre at Causeway Head, with an opening date planned for 1986. Their area of responsibility took in a rural coastline and hinterland populated largely by farmers, with mostly small settlements. A new visitor centre, with high construction costs and a considerable maintenance burden, could have put a strain on ratepayers; but it has proved successful.

The Giant's Causeway Visitor Centre opened in May 1986. It received a mixed package of funding, and it contained a wide range of interpretive material, covering the topics the visitors wanted to know about and much more. There was now a partnership between two bodies: the National Trust, charged with conservation, preservation and access, and the Council, which needed at least to break even on running a visitor centre, car parks and a tourist information service. The Centre has won many awards, and the interpretive section was renewed early in 2000.

Worldwide Recognition

Under a convention adopted in 1972, the United Nations Educational, Scientific and Cultural Organisation (UNESCO) established a list of properties around the world which it considers to have outstanding cultural and natural interest. Periodically they add to this list, employing the Convention's criteria for inclusion.

The Giant's Causeway was nominated for inclusion in 1985 and accepted in 1986, making it Ireland's first World Heritage Site. The whole site includes the Causeway itself and cliffs, headlands and bays from Portnaboe in the west to Benbane Head in the east – a total of seventy-one hectares (175 acres). Thus the Causeway joins other well-known sites in UNESCO's list, including natural phenomena such as the United States of America's Grand Canyon and Australia's Great Barrier Reef, cultural sites such as India's Taj Mahal and England's Durham Cathedral, and, more recently, Ireland's ancient monuments of the Boyne Valley and the island of Skellig Michael off Co Kerry. This important honour was officially celebrated in April 1987, when Magnus Magnusson unveiled a large, suitably inscribed basalt boulder at the Giant's Causeway Centre, and paid a visit to the famous stones to see them for himself.

The Causeway and its surrounding coastline have not been ignored on national and regional levels. In 1987, the Department of the Environment for

Northern Ireland declared the Causeway site – within the same boundaries as the World Heritage site – a National Nature Reserve, acknowledging the importance of its geology and of its flora and fauna. The same Department designated the Causeway Coast Area of Outstanding Natural Beauty in 1989. Details of these designations can be found in Appendix I.

It is important that such accolades and protective designations are understood by residents and visitors. World Heritage status has become better-known since its development in the 1970s, through UNESCO's publicity and educational programmes. A proportion of visitors to the Causeway recognise what this means, as those who are interested and widely travelled may have visited other World Heritage sites.

To those who ask, 'So what?' – and many do – the answers need to have some practical significance. It is not enough to say that the inclusion of the Causeway in this list recognises its geological significance within the natural world and acknowledges the cultural importance of the nearby *Girona* wreck site. Perhaps a better response is to add that the three designations mentioned are important to the owners of the Causeway site – the National Trust – and those in partnership in its management, including Moyle District Council (which owns the Visitor Centre and car parks) and the Department of the Environment (which is involved with nature conservation and the access road). Among other reasons, these designations are important because they are

National Trust workers maintaining the Causeway Coast path.

relevant when help is sought with financing the care and running of the site, and with the production of educational, interpretive and promotional material. It is nice to have letters after your name, but it is better if they do you some good.

Bird on a Wire

We understand complex issues more easily when there is a single case of note, a symbol. On the Causeway Coast, there is one particularly excellent case for a good balance of conservation, agriculture and education – a symbol of the danger of local extinction. This symbol is the rare crow called the chough.

On the Causeway Coast – indeed, in Northern Ireland – the chough is walking a tightrope between survival and extinction. In the year 2000, it is almost losing its balance in this high-wire act: at the time of writing (February 2000), there are only three birds left – all on the north coast.

This handsome, glossy black bird, with its curved red beak and red legs, had its stronghold in Northern Ireland on the Antrim coast, including Rathlin Island. As recently as the 1960s, many cliff nesting-sites were occupied, and wandering flocks of twenty or more birds were regular sights in late summer and through the winter. By 1982, the breeding population was only about ten pairs, and in 1992 only two nesting pairs were found. Now, there is only one pair – which has not bred successfully for several years – on the Causeway cliffs, and a single, lonely bird further east, half of a former breeding pair.

In western Europe, including Ireland's west coast, chough populations are surviving moderately well, particularly where low-key pastoral agriculture, with mixed habitats, exists or is encouraged. Choughs feed mainly on insects, probing for them with their curved beaks in short, well-grazed pastures and around exposed soil on cliffs, slopes or other disturbed ground. These habitats were once widespread around the Antrim and north Derry coastline, and particularly on Rathlin Island. Intensification of agriculture, however, with the use of chemicals to boost grass growth and crop production, has greatly altered the extent of the birds' preferred foraging habitats, and has probably reduced their food supply. These changes in agricultural practices are thought to be the main factor influencing the chough's drastic decline in Northern Ireland. Other factors are the birds' geographical isolation (the nearest other choughs are on Islay, in Scotland, and in Donegal), the role of predators, and competition with other species.

The importance of agriculture has been recognised: the Royal Society for the Protection of Birds and others undertook surveys of the north-coast choughs' behaviour and feeding areas – especially near nesting sites – and, following these

Above: *The chough is a specialist crow which uses its long, curved beak to winkle insects from the soil and close-grazed vegetation along the Causeway cliffs. The bird is now very rare in Northern Ireland.*

Right: *Red campion is a vigorous plant which flowers along this coastline in spring and summer. Here it forms a thick clump under a laterite exposure in one of the Causeway bays.*

Above: *An Easter snowfall turns spring back to winter for these cattle, which are more interested in finding food than in the view of Rathlin Island, in the east, and of the Mull of Kintyre in Scotland.*

Below: *The guesthouses of the popular holiday resort of Portrush cluster along the neck of the volcanic sill of Ramore Head.*

Above: *Shallow water; the grass-capped, eroded coves, caves and arches of the White Rocks near Portrush; and dark volcanic basalt behind.*

Below: *All ages enjoy a summer day by the White Rocks, between Portrush and Dunluce Castle.*

Above: The dramatic remains of Dunluce Castle. The shell of the Jacobean manor house dominates the centre of the site, while the eroded cliff in the foreground is a reminder of a stormy evening in 1639 when the kitchen collapsed into the sea, taking several servants to their deaths.

Below: A quiet day on the unusually shaped convex strand east of Portrush.

Opposite: Between April and September every year, since at least the 1780s, salmon fishermen have slung a precarious rope bridge across the neck of an extinct volcano at Carrick-a-Rede. This gives them access to their nets, and provides a thrill for the thousands of tourists who venture over it each summer.

Above: Kinbane Castle — a hidden gem tucked away in a remote cove at the eastern end of the Causeway Coast.

Below: The shag, or green cormorant, nests on ledges and in caves along the Causeway Coast, often decorating its nest with colourful bits of fishing-net and rope.

Opposite: Portaneevey viewpoint is one of the few places on the mainland from which the remote summer salmon fishery of Carrick-a-Rede can be spotted.

Over: Treasure recovered from the wreck of the Spanish Armada ship Girona.

surveys, the Department of Agriculture for Northern Ireland has taken action. In consultation with conservation organisations, local farmers and other landowners (such as the National Trust), the Department introduced a support scheme to encourage the landowners to maintain 'chough-friendly' feeding habitats, particularly in areas near nesting sites where they are known to feed regularly. Considerable effort is also going into educating people of all ages, stressing the need for sustainable use of the coast and countryside. The case of the chough is a warning to all: the bird is an indicator of a healthy balance between man and the environment, and its decline should tell us something significant.

With so few choughs left in the province, it is touch and go whether this exuberant bird, with its ringing call and aerobatic flight, will continue to grace the Causeway cliffs for much longer.

Sustainable Coastal Management

Today, the partnership has widened: the management of the Giant's Causeway, and of the broader area of the beautiful Derry and Antrim coastline from Magilligan Point to Larne, is becoming a complex mixture of tourism, marketing and management; landscape, building and nature conservation; and many other issues of economic and environmental importance.

There has been no shortage of management plans, strategies and surveys offering opinions on how the overall issue of sustainable coastal management can be addressed and, hopefully, answered. There are plans in hand covering rural transport, interpretation, the carrying capacities of various popular sites, and many other topics; and there are encouraging signs of a more 'bottom-up' approach, involving local communities, than previously existed. There is a proposed Coastal Forum for Northern Ireland, but to date it has not been set up by the government.

Care of the Causeway, and of its surrounding coast, must find ways of maintaining the area's outstanding natural beauty, without allowing necessary developments to stand out. That is the giant challenge.

Rock-fall on the cliff path.

LOCATION OF WALKS AND GIANT'S CAUSEWAY

Dunseverick Walk

Benbane Head

Continuation of
Causeway Coast Path

Giant's Causeway

Runkerry Walk

Causeway
Walk

Dunseverick
Castle

A2

Continuation of
Causeway Coast Path

PORTBALLINTRAE

Dunluce
Castle

BUSHMILLS

1:50,000 Sheet 5 O.S.(N.I.)

LANDSCAPE AND WILDLIFE
Where to go, What to see

WALKING IS THE BEST WAY TO APPRECIATE THE LANDSCAPE AND ITS WILDLIFE. THERE IS PLENTY OF CHOICE AT THE CAUSEWAY. THIS CHAPTER DESCRIBES THREE WALKS AND A LONGER TOUR OF THE NEARBY COASTLINE, WHICH CAN BE UNDERTAKEN ON FOOT, BY BICYCLE OR CAR. ALL BEGIN FROM THE GIANT'S CAUSEWAY CENTRE CAR PARKS, EXCEPT FOR THE TOUR, WHICH STARTS AT PORTRUSH.

The aim of the walks and the tour is to encourage exploration of landscape and wildlife, recommending stops at various vantage points or sites of interest. The combination of landscape, habitats and wildlife gives the walker a feeling for the ecology of the area – the ways in which the living things relate to their environment. A bit of local history is slipped in, too, for humans have their own ecology. The walks and the tour follow waymarked paths and signposted roads, and are designed to enable you to see features of the landscape, the variety of habitats and their flora and fauna, without leaving the safety of the paths or roads, which also avoids disturbance.

The emphasis below is on spring and summer, the times when the wildflowers are at their best, birds are breeding and most visitors come to see the Causeway. Autumn and winter have their own beauty, and the Causeway in stormy conditions is a sight to remember – although it should be viewed from a cautious distance!

Information panel for walkers at the Giant's Causeway.

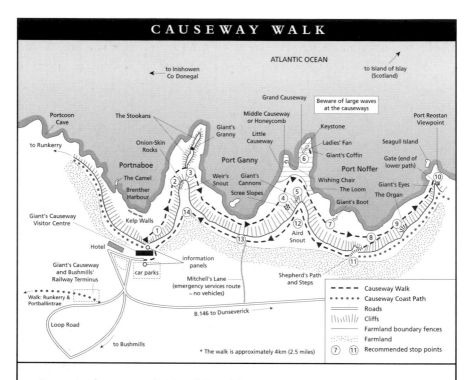

CAUSEWAY WALK

ATLANTIC OCEAN

to Inishowen
Co Donegal

to Island of Islay
(Scotland)

Grand Causeway

Beware of large waves
at the causeways

Portcoon
Cave

The Stookans

Middle Causeway
or Honeycomb

Port Reostan
Viewpoint

Giant's
Granny

Keystone

Onion-Skin
Rocks

Little
Causeway

Ladies' Fan

Seagull Island

to Runkerry

Portnaboe

Port Ganny

Giant's Coffin

Gate (end of
lower path)

The Camel

Weir's
Snout

Giant's
Cannons

Port Noffer

Brenther
Harbour

Scree Slopes

Wishing Chair

Giant's Eyes

The Loom

The Organ

Giant's Causeway
Visitor Centre

Kelp Walls

Giant's Boot

Hotel

Aird
Snout

Giant's Causeway
and Bushmills'
Railway Terminus

car parks

information
panels

Mitchell's Lane
(emergency services route
– no vehicles)

Shepherd's Path
and Steps

Walk: Runkerry &
Portballintrae

B.146 to Dunseverick

Loop Road

to Bushmills

* The walk is approximately 4km (2.5 miles)

- - - - Causeway Walk
•••••• Causeway Coast Path
===== Roads
|\||\\// Cliffs
——— Farmland boundary fences
Farmland
⑦ ⑪ Recommended stop points

Start: At the seaward side of the Visitor Centre.

Finish: Same place (this is a circular walk).

Distance: About 4 kilometres (2.5 miles).

Time: Allow 1.5 to 2 hours, including stops.

Terrain: Surfaced paths, varying from tarmac to stones over soil, uneven in places. Steep stone steps (about 150) linking walk from sea level to cliff-top. Bus available (charge) between Visitor Centre and Causeway, with facilities for wheelchair users (type of transport may vary).

Safety: Steep downhill section at the start of the walk; the Causeway itself is uneven, with some loose rocks. Beware of large waves and unfenced drops at the Causeway. The cliff-top path should be avoided in high winds. The cliff edges can be unstable, so keep to the paths. If the steps are intimidating, you can simply return the way you came, shortening the walk considerably.

Information: Information panels in the main car park and at the start of the walk, by the road.

Maps: Map 4 or 5 of the Ordnance Survey NI 1:50,000 *Discoverer* series. See sketch map in this chapter for general guidance only.

This walk can be done in either direction, but here it is set out in a clockwise direction, taking you down the hill to the Causeway first. If you prefer to walk down the Shepherd's Steps rather than up, reverse the direction and go along the cliff-top path first (obviously you will have to read this guide differently).

From the **Start**, walk about 100 metres down the hill in front of you to **Stop 1, Portnaboe**. This stop is beside the obvious orange-red exposure of laterite, the crumbly inter-basaltic bed containing iron ore, which is overlaid at the uphill end by glacial deposits of clay and stones. Looking down into the bay on your left (Portnaboe), note the small, spring-fed reed bed near the rocky shore, and the clumps of bramble and bracken amongst the grass and ferns. These are good habitats for birds which spend the spring and summer here, such as grasshopper warblers and whitethroats – rather nondescript and elusive brown warblers – the former with a churring song like the sound of a sewing machine, the latter a more tuneful songster. Sometimes a brown-and-grey hawk, the kestrel, hovers overhead, searching the ground for small prey. Tucked under the cliffs is the Camel Rock, a hard basalt dyke which does look like a camel crouched down; beyond it, fulmars glide to and from their rocky nest

sites. Large eider ducks are often seen bobbing on the sea and resting on the small islands; the males are black and white, and the females are brown. A loud, piping call helps to identify oyster-catchers, black-and-white wading birds which frequent the rocky shore. The low stone walls near the tideline were part of the kelp industry, which died out around the 1930s; seaweed was gathered in winter and spring and spread on these walls to dry, then burned to produce residues rich in useful mineral salts.

The narrow, humped back of the Camel, a hard dyke of rock.

Stop 2. Onion-skin rocks. At the bottom of the hill, on the right, large rounded boulders are set, like currants in a cake, in the purple-red patch of an inter-basaltic bed. These big stones are weathering gradually in layers – hence the name 'onion-skin' rocks. Erosion often loosens them, so keep your distance.

Stop 3. Windy Gap. This is the point where the road continues around the corner, and it is worth a pause; it gives you a wonderful first view (and a photo opportunity) of the Giant's Causeway in

Weathered rocks, known as the 'Onion-skins'.

the foreground, with the towering cliffs and isolated pillars of the Chimneys beyond. On a clear day, the higher parts of the Scottish island of Islay are visible on the horizon. You are now in Port Ganny, the only Causeway bay with a little sand. The steep hills on the seaward side of the gap are the Stookans, so called because their shape resembles that of corn stooks. The thin vegetation and poor soils are easily disturbed, so please avoid the temptation to climb. The pale blue vernal squill – a scarce and beautiful spring plant, closely related to the bluebell, with delicate star-shaped flowers – blooms here in May and June; it is easily seen from the base of the Stookans.

Stop 4. The Little Causeway. The path divides here, a short loop (optional) taking you down past the columns of the Little Causeway and back to the road. The loose stones on the hillside – scree – are typical of the lower slopes of these unstable cliffs. The terrain is inhospitable to plants; nevertheless, in May and June you may see herb Robert (pink, with green or red leaves) and pink-and-white, fleshy-leafed English stonecrop in flower amongst these stones. Look out for ravens – large crows with a deep croak – along the cliffs behind you. The agile, reddish Irish stoat is sometimes seen dashing over these screes.

Stop 5. The Giant's Cannons. Poking out of the lower side of the hill are tilted Causeway columns. Vegetation has masked these somewhat. In earlier times they were known as the Giant's Cannons. The slopes above are extremely unstable; do not climb on them.

Stop 6. The Honeycomb (Middle) and Grand Causeways. The Middle and Grand Causeways will thrill you with a memorable impression of how precisely the columns fit together. Note the predominance of five- and six-sided columns. Lichens grow over the Causeway in distinct zones: they are grey near the centre, then vivid yellow, and close to the sea they form a thin black coating, which is often mistaken for oil pollution. Fanciful names – the Wishing Chair, the Keystone, the Giant's Coffin, the Lady's Fan and so on – have been given to some of the arrangements of stones on the Causeways; some are marked on the map for this walk, but a guide is needed to locate most of them. A small buff bird with a white tail is often seen here in summer; this is the wheatear, which manages to raise a brood of young amongst the stones and the numerous visitors before flying south to Africa for the winter. From the Causeway, you can see the Giant's Granny (imagination required!), a bent old lady of stone, on the left-hand side of the Stookans opposite. In spring and summer, the gaps between the

A male wheatear – a summer visitor to the rocky Causeway area.

Causeway stones are bright with wild flowers such as sea pink, white sea campion and more of the pale-blue vernal squill. Offshore, seabirds such as large white gannets pass by, and you might spot an Atlantic grey seal in the water. Looking east across Port Noffer, note the various layers of basalts (lava flows), more reddish soils exposed halfway up, and the remarkable pipe-like columns of the Organ.

Stop 7. The Giant's Boot. This is a large rock about 200 metres past the Causeway, in Port Noffer, sitting where the grass meets the rocky shore. Like the Granny, it is best seen from a particular angle – in this case, from the first wooden seat you come to along the path; from this point, it does indeed resemble a huge hiking boot. From its size, it has been calculated that its owner, Finn MacCool, the giant, was sixteen metres (fifty-two feet six inches) tall! This ice- and sea-hewn boulder is marked on maps as the Giant's Chair, but you need to sit on it to realise why! The nearby marshy ground is a fragile habitat for summer-flowering yellow flag iris and spotted orchids, which do not like to be trampled – enjoy them from the Boot or the path.

Stop 8. Port Noffer. The name means 'the Giant's Port'; it is the large bay extending from the Causeway to the headland with the distinctive pinnacles of the Chimneys. Springs and freshwater seepage from the slopes feed this marshy area. In spring and summer, reed buntings, wrens, and sedge and grasshopper warblers call and sing from the reed bed. The dark, wall-like projections of rock on the shore are hard basalt dykes. The

A dark band of lichen around the edge of the Giant's Causeway.

shady slopes and cliffs above support woodland-like vegetation, including primroses, violets, wood anemones and woodrush.

Stop 9. The Organ. To reach this, continue along the path in Port Noffer, following it as it rises gradually (at this stage, ignore the sharp right-hand turn halfway up; the walk will bring you back to this). The Organ, which dominates the cliff ahead, is a spectacular group of basalt columns about twelve metres (forty feet) high, with remarkably even cross-fractures giving a building-blocks effect. Grey-green lichen clings to the exposed surfaces. The colonnade changes abruptly to the less regular entablature above. From this viewpoint, enjoy the east prospect of the Giant's Causeway, with the Stookans in the middle distance. The Inishowen peninsula of Co Donegal, running north into the Atlantic, is visible in good weather. You can choose to turn back here and head towards the steps to the cliff-top (see below), or you can continue about 500 metres to the next stop, which is as far as this part of the path goes.

Stop 10. Port Reostan viewpoint. The cliff face next to the path consists of red, purple and grey forms of laterite. The oval hollows in this are made by weathered rocks falling out, leaving sockets known as the Giant's Eyes. A few retain their cores of crumbling basalt. The gate you reach at the end of this path was erected in 1994, following severe collapses of the cliff-faces beyond. You can see the remains of a path beyond the gate, but it is very unsafe, so do *not* go any further. This is where you must retrace your steps to the turn in the path mentioned above; by taking the left-hand fork, you will reach the Shepherd's Steps to the cliff-top.

Stop 11. Shepherd's Path and Steps (150+). This path between cliff-top and sea was once used by shepherds and seaweed-gatherers. Halfway up, pause to rest, for the climb is steep. In spring, this is a chance to enjoy the profusion of primroses, violets and early purple orchids on the steep grassy hillside. Later, in summer, the cream flowers of meadowsweet and angelica are buzzing with insects. At the top, the farmed landscape inland is home to fewer wildflowers; but in winter, the barley stubble and damp grassy fields support flocks of whooper swans and geese. Much smaller birds may be sharing these fields: flocks of buff and white snow buntings, twittering brown linnets, and twites, which are similar to linnets but can be distinguished by their twanging call. The birdwatcher's jargon for such easily confused species is 'LBJs' – 'Little Brown Jobs'.

Stop 12. Aird Snout. At the cliff-top, a right turn begins your walk back to the Visitor Centre. The next headland is Aird Snout, which overlooks the Causeway. The black-lichen zone is particularly obvious from here. The small patch of dry heath behind the snout is a rare habitat, purple with heaths and heather in summer, dotted with the pink-and-white flowers of cat's-paw, an uncommon species. From March to June, the gorse along the path in this area is vivid with yellow flowers.

Stop 14. Mitchell's Lane. The fields on either side of this farm lane (the only one along this section of the path) are part of the National Trust's farming and conservation work. Heathland regeneration is encouraged by limiting fertiliser use and controlling grazing. Rabbits help to keep the sward close-cropped, and they share the shelter of the gorse clumps with sheep and small birds such as wrens (tiny and brown, with a loud, rattling song) and black-headed, russet-breasted stonechats (named after their call, which sounds like two pebbles being chipped together).

The stonechat, a resident bird of the Causeway Coast.

Stop 15. Weir's Snout. Another narrow headland, and the next good viewpoint. Salty winds and winter grazing keep the grass in the field beside the headland at just the right length to produce a rich growth of wildflowers, including pale-pink meadow thistles, in spring and summer. The Northern Ireland Department of Agriculture encourages landowners in this work through the Environmentally Sensitive Areas scheme.

If you complete this walk and are lucky with the weather, the views and the wildlife, you will have had a good introduction to the Giant's Causeway and its natural history. If you just wander along, head down and perhaps chatting to friends, it still should be an enjoyable experience.

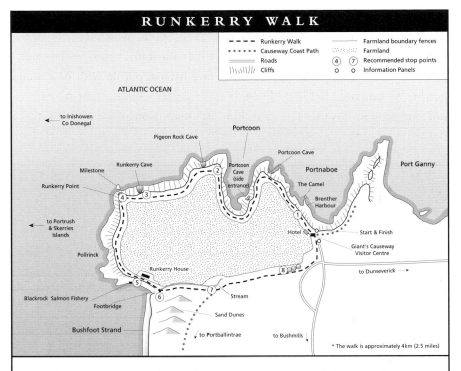

RUNKERRY WALK

Legend:
- – – – Runkerry Walk
- • • • • Causeway Coast Path
- ═══ Roads
- |\|\|/|/ Cliffs
- ─── Farmland boundary fences
- Farmland
- ④ ⑦ Recommended stop points
- ○ ○ Information Panels

ATLANTIC OCEAN

to Inishowen Co Donegal

Pigeon Rock Cave

Portcoon

Portcoon Cave

Runkerry Cave

Portcoon Cave (side entrance)

Portnaboe

Port Ganny

Milestone

The Camel

Runkerry Point

Brenther Harbour

to Portrush & Skerries Islands

Hotel

Start & Finish

Giant's Causeway Visitor Centre

Pollrinck

to Dunseverick

Runkerry House

Blackrock Salmon Fishery

Footbridge

Stream

Bushfoot Strand

Sand Dunes

to Portballintrae

to Bushmills

* The walk is approximately 4km (2.5 miles)

Start: At the seaward side of the Visitor Centre. Turn left; the walk begins along the cliff.

Finish: In the same place (another circular walk).

Distance: 4 kilometres (2.5 miles).

Time: Allow 1.5 hours, including stops.

Terrain: Begins and ends on surfaced paths, but much of the cliff-top section is grassy and slippery when wet. There are some steps, at least two gates and a footbridge over a small stream.

Safety: The cliff-top walk is not recommended in very strong winds. From the sand rodden back towards the Visitor Centre, a small railway train may sometimes be in operation alongside the path. The caves are inaccessible except by boat, except for Portcoon's side entrance, where care is needed, especially at high tide. Beware of large waves.

Information: There are information panels in the Visitor Centre's main car park and at the start of the walk.

Maps: Map 4 or Map 5 of the Ordnance Survey NI *Discoverer* 1:50,000 series. See sketch map in this chapter for general guidance only.

Stop 1. Portnaboe. Follow the cliff-top path past the rear of the Causeway hotel; Stop 1, above Portnaboe, is about 200 metres along, where you have a good view down into the bay on your right. The name means 'Port of the Cow', perhaps because this bay was once grazed by stock. The small harbour used to be a popular location for boat trips to see the caves and the Causeway, but this tradition died out in the 1940s, although there is a possibility that it may be revived. The leaning, humped rock just beyond the Brenther harbour is a dyke, where lava forced its way up from deep in the earth through a crack; because of its shape, it is called the Camel. Portcoon Cave, the first of three, lies a little to the west, at a break in the rock platforms, but access is by a side entrance further along this walk. Ravens and

The fulmar, a noticeable cliff-dwelling bird.

kestrels are sometimes seen along this section, and there are good views of the noisy grey-and-white fulmars which occupy the cliffs. Plants of the shoreline include the sweet-smelling, white-flowered scurvy grass; its fleshy leaves are rich in Vitamin C, which prevents scurvy, an unpleasant condition affecting anyone deprived of this vitamin. Long ago, the plant was collected by sailors, who ran short of fresh fruit and vegetables on long voyages.

Stop 2. Portcoon. The name means 'the narrow port or inlet'. A side entrance to Portcoon Cave is visible opposite this stop. From inside the cave, the sound of the swell rumbling on the boulders and the view of the sea through the Gothic-arched entrance add to the atmosphere of this little-known part of the Causeway, visited in the past by boatloads of nervous tourists.

Stop 3. Runkerry Cave. To see the cave entrance, you need to approach – with care – the grassy edge on the Causeway side. The green and pink algae coating the sea-washed cave walls, and the shiny green fronds of hart's-tongue fern above, give colour to this otherwise sombre cave entrance. Rock doves (ancestors of the common pigeon) and shags (also known as green cormorants) nest inside, and flocks of starlings whir in at dusk to a safe roost. Like all three caves, Runkerry narrows gradually as it runs deep into this headland. Along the base of these cliffs run wave-cut rock platforms, where eiders sometimes sit and a few herring gulls nest.

Stop 4. Runkerry Point. A good viewpoint, looking west to the Skerries islands, Portrush and Co Donegal. The name 'Runkerry' has been interpreted as 'the promontory of the pillar stones'. The projecting lump of rock just off this headland, often occupied by shags, is a well-known fisherman's sea marker known as the Milestone. On the headland, look for the horizontal cracks typical of a dyke. The cinder-like gravel and bare black rock here give an idea of how barren this coastline would have been after the lava flows cooled, and the little green rosettes of buck's-horn plantain (so named because the leaves are serrated like a stag's horn) cling tenaciously to this harsh habitat. Black guillemots live around these cliffs – plump, sooty birds with a white flash on each wing. Their thin, reedy calls can sometimes be heard, and if you look at them on the water you may notice their vermilion legs and feet.

Stop 5. Runkerry House. This imposing house, with its crow-stepped gables, was originally built in 1883 for Lord Macnaghten, whose family is still

Runkerry House.

associated with nearby Bushmills. Lord Macnaghten's daughters lived here for many years; when the family no longer required the house, it became a home for the elderly, then an outdoor training centre. In 1998-99, under new ownership, it was renovated and new sections were added in the same style, to provide luxury private apartments. The building is made of sandstone, which takes on a warm glow in the evening sun. The small slipway and the poles for hanging nets belong to Blackrock Salmon Fishery, which has not operated for a decade or so as part of the River Bush salmon conservation study. Some of the largest waves along this coast roll into the bay, and when the river is high, a brown, peaty stain of fresh water can be seen across the sea's surface.

Stop 6. Runkerry footbridge. The little stream tumbling over rocks to the sea attracts birds such as grey wagtails, yellow below and grey on top. The exposed glacial clays and sandbanks on the beach side of the bridge are riddled with small holes, the nesting sites of sand martins, small, brown, swallow-like birds; look out for them between March and September. This corner of Blackrock Strand is often full of flotsam and jetsam from the sea, including tangles of the brown seaweed, or wrack, once used in the kelp industry, as described above.

Stop 7. The Sand Rodden. The rodden – a local name for a rough track – runs from the public road to the beach. A little inland from the dunes, it meets the tram track along which the Causeway tram trundled between 1887 and 1949. In the scrub, willow warblers and whitethroats sing in spring, and at any time you might hear the squeal of a water rail, a secretive, grey-brown water bird, from the depths of the swamp. Wild leeks, red campion, primroses and bluebells are spring treats along the edges of this little stream, in the shade of the trees.

Stop 8. Sycamore copse. Woodland is very scarce on the Causeway coast. Rooks take advantage of these few trees to nest, and are noisily engaged in domestic life from March to June. Between here and the Causeway Centre, you cross the Runkerry Road and pass the former Causeway tram terminus. This is where the new Giant's Causeway and Bushmills Railway will drop visitors taking a ride along part of the older tram route.

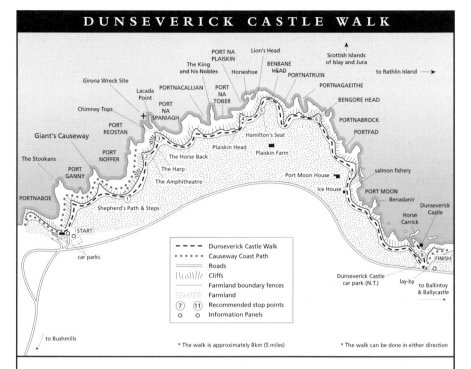

DUNSEVERICK CASTLE WALK

Lion's Head
PORT NA PLAISKIN
Scottish Islands of Islay and Jura
The King and his Nobles
BENBANE HEAD
Horseshoe
PORTNATRUIN
to Rathlin Island →
Girona Wreck Site
PORTNACALLIAN
PORT NA TOBER
PORTNAGAEITHE
Lacada Point
BENGORE HEAD
Chimney Tops
PORT NA SPANIAGH
PORTNABROCK
PORT REOSTAN
PORTFAD
Giant's Causeway
Hamilton's Seat
The Stookans
PORT NOFFER
Plaiskin Head
Plaiskin Farm
PORTNABOE
PORT GANNY
The Horse Back
The Harp
Port Moon House
salmon fishery
The Amphitheatre
Ice House
PORT MOON
Benadanir
Shepherd's Path & Steps
Dunseverick Castle
Horse Carrick
START
car parks
FINISH
Dunseverick Castle car park (N.T.)
lay-by
to Ballintoy & Ballycastle
to Bushmills

- - - - Dunseverick Castle Walk
• • • • • Causeway Coast Path
Roads
Cliffs
Farmland boundary fences
Farmland
(7) (11) Recommended stop points
o   o   Information Panels

* The walk is approximately 8km (5 miles)   * The walk can be done in either direction

Start: At the seaward side of the Visitor Centre; take the way-marked cliff-top path.

Finish: At Dunseverick Castle; the path meets the B146 road at a lay-by.

Distance: 8 kilometres (5 miles). If you return by road, it is shorter: 4.5 kilometres (2.8 miles).

Time: Allow at least 3 hours, including stops. It is a good plan to have transport parked at Dunseverick Castle, if possible, to bring you back; or check the bus schedule for Ulsterbus service 172 between Ballycastle and Portrush. There is a lay-by and a car park with picnic tables.

Terrain: Surfaced path until a little way beyond the Shepherd's Steps, then grassy for the rest of the walk; in wet weather, it can be very muddy and slippery in places. There are some steps and stiles along the route.

Safety: Not recommended in high winds. Keep well clear of cliff edges, as these are undercut by erosion in many places.

Information: There are information panels in the main car park of the Visitor Centre, at the start of the walk and in the lay-by opposite Dunseverick Castle. Because the cliffs are high, reaching a maximum of 114 metres (374 feet), binoculars are helpful in spotting some of the features mentioned.

From the *Start*, follow the cliff-top path to the top of the Shepherd's Steps. You can refer to the Causeway walk in reverse (Stops 14 back to 11) for information on this section.

Stop 1 (11 on the Causeway Walk). Shepherd's Steps. Instead of descending the steps, continue east along the cliff-top. On the way to the next stop, you will pass another small area of dry heath, where you may see the stonechat, a bird typical of this coastline. Most of the fenced-off, rough, grazing land extending to the road is owned and managed as a nature conservation area by the National Trust. You may spot some large, russet Irish hares.

Stop 2. The Amphitheatre Bay. From the narrow promontory of Roveran Valley Head, the fine colonnades of the middle basalts are visible on the upper half of the cliffs. The red bed of laterite towards the far point is pitted with Giant's Eyes, almond-shaped cores of partly weathered basalt, most of which are empty sockets where these basalts have fallen out. Over a hundred pairs of fulmars find the columns ideal as nesting sites, and the birds glide about the deep bay on updrafts of air. In spring and summer, the slopes are yellow with kidney vetch and bird's-foot trefoil. The Amphitheatre is prone to major landslides, the scars of which are quite obvious, and what is left of the lower path – now closed permanently – is littered with rock and soil debris.

Stop 3. Chimney Tops. Eighteenth- and nineteenth-century prints show more pillars than now exist; those which remain are isolated from the cliff-face by erosion. Curving into the sea below is Lacada Point, which means 'long flagstone'. It was here the *Girona* foundered on 26 October 1588; when its treasures were recovered in 1967-69, they were mostly found under the stones and boulders of the seabed, at a depth of around ten metres (just over thirty feet), on either side of this point. In Port na Spaniagh Bay, there is a long dyke of dark basalt running into the sea, near which lie the rusting remains of an old navigation buoy (nothing to do with the Armada). The eastern end of this bay shows a purple-blue exposure of the inter-basaltic bed, containing silica, with redder iron ore above.

Stop 4. Plaiskin Head. Leaving Port na Spaniagh, you pass the dipped ridge of The Horseback, the sides of which have many wavy columns. In spring and summer the grassy slopes of these bays are full of wildflowers, including red campion – with many of its colour variations, through pink to white – and look out for clumps of sea pink and the white flowers of sea campion. The cliff-edge vegetation in summer includes creeping willow, the purple devil's-bit scabious and creamy burnet rose. At Plaiskin, there is a chance to see peregrine falcons and perhaps the very rare chough (pronounced 'chuff'), a glossy crow with red legs and beak and a ringing call.

Stop 5. Hamilton's Seat. Before arriving at Hamilton's Seat – which has a name plaque beside waymarks – notice the horseshoe cove below, and, in the reddish laterite well up the cliff-face, a distinctively shaped projection known as the Lion's Head. At Hamilton's Seat, take time to admire the view back to the west, taking in Plaiskin Head in the foreground and the rugged coastline beyond.

The 'horseshoe' cove below Hamilton's Seat.

The lava flows of the east side of Plaiskin Head are the finest along the whole coast. Natural erosion in the red layer is undermining one of the colonnades of pillars, near the point of the headland. At sea level, the surface of the lower basalts is a crazy-paving of Causeway-like shapes. Choughs, peregrine falcons and kestrels might put in an appearance while you enjoy this fine landscape.

Stop 6. Bengore Head. The name means 'Peak of the Goats', but it is sheep you may see here, precariously balanced on narrow tracks around the headlands, ever searching for that extra little bit of vegetation to nibble. From Bengore, the cliffs drop in height as they progress eastwards, with the Causeway basalts meeting the white chalk at Portbraddan, by White Park Bay. The view from Bengore towards the Mull of Kintyre in Scotland includes Sheep Island off Ballintoy, Rathlin Island, Fair Head and the island of Sanda off Kintyre, with the cone of Ailsa Craig beyond. Many of the gannets seen offshore nest on this great lump of granite.

Stop 7. Port Moon. The northern grassy promontory of this long bay looks down on Port Fad. From the tip of the point, the entrance to a nineteenth-century bauxite mine can be seen. These old mines are very dangerous and should not be entered. Port Moon has a long history of salmon fishing, and the little red-roofed fishery cottage looks out on a bag net, fished from May through August. It is said that tea brewed from spring water here will turn milk blue, due to the high copper content of the water. On the stony beaches towards Dunseverick Castle are a few low kelp walls. Across the bay is the jagged profile of Benadanir ('Peak of the Danes'), a favourite perch for peregrine falcons. Buzzards are sometimes seen riding the air currents along the cliffs. As you leave Port Moon, you pass the fishery ice house, long disused, tucked in amidst the gorse on the inland side of the fence-line by the stone steps.

Stop 8. Dunseverick Castle. Fulmars are numerous along the cliffs towards the castle. The Horse Carrick islet below the castle promontory – its shape speaks for itself – may have shags and eiders around it. The ancient fortified promontory of Dunseverick, with the scant remains of the castle, can be reached by steps and a narrow track. Most historians agree that this defensive site has a long history of occupation, possibly going back to pre-Christian times. It was reputedly the end of one of the great early-Christian roads from Tara, and was almost certainly the capital of the Celtic kingdom of Dalriada. Legends claim that St Patrick visited the site. The castle – what remains of it – is more recent. In the sixteenth and seventeenth centuries, it was occupied by a branch of the Ulster O'Cahan family; in the 1640s the O'Cahans lost possession of the castle, and in about 1653 it was destroyed by Cromwellian troops. The ruins visible today were part of the gatehouse. Beyond Dunseverick, to the east, you can see the landscape change to lower headlands and the wide sandy sweep of White Park Bay, backed by slumped chalk cliffs. You have reached the end of the Causeway bays and headlands.

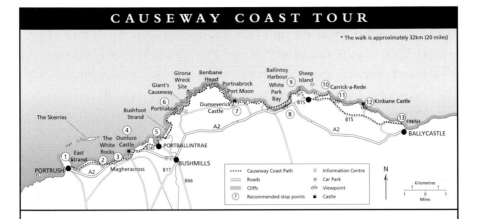

CAUSEWAY COAST TOUR

* The walk is approximately 32km (20 miles)

Map labels: Girona Wreck Site, Benbane Head, Ballintoy Harbour, Sheep Island, Giant's Causeway, Portnabrock, Port Moon, White Park Bay, Carrick-a-Rede, Portnaboe, Dunseverick Castle, Bushfoot Strand, The Skerries, East Strand, The White Rocks, Dunluce Castle, PORTBALLINTRAE, Kinbane Castle, B15, A2, FINISH, BALLYCASTLE, PORTRUSH, Magheracross, BUSHMILLS, B17, B66, B145, B146

Legend:
- Causeway Coast Path
- Roads
- Cliffs
- Recommended stop points
- Information Centre
- Car Park
- Viewpoint
- Castle

N

Kilometres / Miles

Start: At the large car park on the east side of Ramore Head, Portrush.

Finish: At Ballycastle sea-front.

Distance: About 32 kilometres (20 miles) by main roads, excluding detours. It is 42 kilometres (27 miles) if walked by the Causeway Coast Path.

Time: At least one day's walk. An energetic day's cycling. An easy run – about half a day – by car.

Terrain: Metalled roads all the way: the A2 from Portrush, diverting to Portballintrae along the B145, back to the A2 through Bushmills, then to the B146 Causeway Road, which rejoins the A2 beyond Dunseverick. Go through Ballintoy on the B15; this will take you along the coast to Ballycastle. There are car parks, lay-bys, picnic sites and toilets reasonably spaced along the route. Cyclists following the recommended route 93 will be diverted along some attractive minor roads. Walkers can follow the way-marked Causeway Coast Path; about two-thirds of this is off-road, following coastal paths.

Maps: Maps 4 and 5 of the Ordnance Survey NI 1:50,000 *Discoverer* series. The map at the end of this chapter is for general guidance only.

In 1989, the Causeway Coast was designated an Area of Outstanding Natural Beauty by the Department of the Environment for Northern Ireland. The AONB, as it is known, extends from Portrush in the west to Ballycastle in the east, along a narrow strip of coastal land covering 4,200 hectares (10,380 acres). It is a diverse landscape of cliff and beach; both coast and hinterland have been occupied by humans for over seven thousand years. The area is quite intensively farmed, and there are few trees except for plantations and shelter-belts around homesteads.

This tour, like the walks, emphasises landscape and natural history. Users with other interests – such as local history, archaeology, architecture, or more detailed geology – will find further information through the Bibliography, and on outdoor panels at most car parks and some viewpoints.

Start: Ramore Head car park, Portrush. Ramore Head, which has been declared an Area of Special Scientific Interest (ASSI) because of its geology, is the culmination of a narrow sill of hard dolerite – an intruded volcanic rock – around which the holiday resort of Portrush has developed. The two sandy beaches, to the west and the east, have contributed to the resort's popularity. The lava forced up from the earth to create Ramore Head also made the little archipelago of islands offshore, known as the Skerries. Like most of the nearby Causeway headlands, these are tilted, with rugged, stepped cliffs facing the Atlantic breakers, while the spray-splashed land behind slopes gently away from the sea. Along the low, rocky shoreline facing the east strand is the National Nature Reserve, which contains the famous 'Portrush rock', source of eighteenth-century hot debates on the origin of basalt. More information is available at the nearby Portrush Countryside Centre.

GIANT'S HEAD, WHITEROCKS, PORTRUSH.

The Giant's Head – chalk cliffs near Portrush.

Stop 2: Whiterocks car park. Whiterocks is also a geological ASSI. Walk the short distance down to the beach, past the information panels, to view the sea-eroded chalk cliffs. The Giant's Head stands out a little to the east, and close inspection of the chalk outcrops along the Whiterocks end of the beach will show bands of brown flints and occasional bullet-like fossils. These are belemnites, an extinct relative of the squid. The unusual convex shape of the long beach between Portrush and here is due to wave refraction by the Skerries islands, which affects the way the sea sculpts this shoreline. Various methods of erosion control have been tried here, with golfers particularly anxious to protect the championship course behind the mobile dunes. Green-and-red burnet moths and banded snails live amongst the sharp marram grass.

Stop 3: Magheracross car park and viewpoint. It is worth pausing at this excellent vantage point, with its information panels. Looking back towards Portrush, there is another good view of the pillars and arches of the eroded chalk cliffs. In May and June, many salt-tolerant plants brighten the grassy slopes by the road and the cliff ledges: sea pink, red campion, white sea campion, scurvy grass, yellow kidney vetch, purple thyme and, here and there on the cliffs, the shiny green leaves of sea beet. In winter, up to four hundred curlews feed in the damp fields across the road. Look east towards Dunluce Castle, and note the change to dark basalt, with the Causeway headlands beyond.

Stop 4: Dunluce Castle. A tour of this, the most spectacular north-coast castle, is a pleasant diversion. The promontory has been occupied for about 1,500 years, since the Iron Age, and the first castle was built by the Normans around AD1300. The castle contains the remains of a Jacobean manor house, and the site was home to MacQuillans and McDonnells before it was abandoned in 1660. The McDonnells improved the castle with an unexpected windfall, which they gathered from the Spanish Armada treasure ship *Girona* after it sank in 1588 near the Giant's Causeway. Ravens and peregrine falcons, suitably noble birds, inhabit this famous ruin and its imposing cliffs.

Stop 5: Portballintrae Beach car park. A diversion down the Bayhead Road (B145) to Portballintrae, a short distance from Dunluce Castle, is worthwhile. In the 1930s, the horseshoe crescent of the bay was lined by a broad sandy beach; but sea erosion carried most of the sand away, and by the 1980s there was no more than you see today. Erosion continues – note the many examples of

Atlantic swell at Bushfoot Strand.

reinforcement and protection needed to keep the houses safe from collapse. As one local resident commented, even his woodworms wear lifejackets! The variety of shore habitats – soil and gravel exposures, rock, seaweed and a little sand – attract a rich variety of birds. In summer, sand martins nest in the eroded sandbanks and white sandwich terns call noisily as they fish in the bay. Winter provides up to ten species of wader: silvery-grey sanderlings, brown ringed plovers, turnstones (mottled brown waders which flip over pebbles and seaweed in search of food), slate-coloured purple sandpipers and others feed and roost between the bay and the mouth of the River Bush, below the car park at the end of the shore road. This is a good place to see surfers in action, as some of the biggest waves on the coast roll in year-round, given unsettled conditions offshore. Occasional porpoises also enjoy the surf.

Stop 6: Giant's Causeway Centre car parks. Motorists have to double back from Stop 5, passing through Bushmills, to reach the Causeway. Walkers and cyclists can cross the footbridge at the mouth of the River Bush and join the Tram Track route to Stop 6. The woodlands surrounding Dundarave Estate outside

Bushmills are private. They are an important refuge for woodland birds on this otherwise rather treeless coast; summer-visiting blackcaps and chiffchaffs lurk here, and one or two pairs of buzzards nest within, cruising on broad wings over the surrounding fields to hunt rabbits. Routes around the Causeway are described above. The Visitor Centre provides a wealth of information on the Causeway Coast, and the shop stocks a good range of books, leaflets and other goods.

Stop 7: Dunseverick Castle car park. The car park on the cliff side of the cottage has picnic tables, and more room than the lay-by. The lay-by has a useful information panel on the wall. Dunseverick, like Dunluce, is a stone castle on a strategic cliff-bound promontory. Little of the original castle remains, but, as the panel describes, this site has a long history of occupation and strife. Rock doves and jackdaws often lurk on the castle walls, constantly exposed to the threat of attack by peregrine falcons. In early summer, the wet hollow below the castle is bright with yellow flag irises. The Scottish islands of Islay and Jura – Islay in front, the hills of Jura behind – lie offshore to the north, and Rathlin Island's black-and-white cliffs, once likened to a drowned magpie, can be seen closer to the Antrim coast.

Stop 8: White Park Bay. There are two viewpoints – the car park by the Youth hostel (medium size) and a lay-by just east of this (small). The lay-by has the better view, taking in the sandy sweep of the bay from the top of the chalk cliffs. The lumpy profile of the grasslands is due to slumped blocks of chalk, which sit uneasily on slippery Lias clay. These fossil-rich clay beds are occasionally exposed in streams and on the lower shore. One of the mounds directly below the lay-by, partially ringed with stones, is a Neolithic burial site, a reminder of occupation of the bay about 5,000 years ago. White Park Bay is another ASSI, with its interesting land forms and scarce plants such as adder's tongue, moonwort – said to cause horses to cast a shoe if they step on it – and many species of orchids.

Stop 9: Ballintoy Harbour. The harbour is reached by the windy road that passes the white Ballintoy church and the extraordinary architecture of Ben Dhu House, built by an artist; the design of this house has prompted one purist to describe it as a construction 'of staggering eccentricity and inappropriateness'. In the nineteenth century the harbour was used to export limestone products, and the lime kilns at the car park dominate this picturesque place. Faulting has

Disused limekilns at Ballintoy Harbour.

created a moonscape of jumbled and tilted basalt sea stacks, dropping them below the level of the older chalk cliffs. The coves are a haven for eider ducks, oystercatchers and other waders; in spring and summer, wildflowers – blue vernal squill, pale-yellow kidney vetch, mauve rock spurrey and purple thyme – cling to the rock stacks. From the pier, nesting cormorants and other seabirds on Sheep Island can be seen just offshore, with the high cliffs of the west end of Rathlin Island further out. From the white church, you can walk to Larrybane, at the entrance to the next site, along a field and cliff-top path with fine views.

Stop 10: Carrick-a-Rede. Carrick-a-Rede is signposted just east of Ballintoy village, on the curve of the road up Knocksoghey Hill. There is a spectacular cliff-top walk from the car park to Carrick-a-Rede, which is the largest of three islands close to the shore. For six months of the year, the nearest island is joined to the mainland by a swinging rope bridge, which is erected by salmon fishermen in mid-April and dismantled at the end of September. Visitors may cross this bridge; some do, some do not, and once in a while someone's nerve fails after the crossing to the island, and he or she refuses to make the return journey – a situation which may require the valuable time of rescue service personnel. Common sense dictates that if you are uneasy about the crossing, you should not cross. National Trust staff are on site daily, during normal opening hours, to advise visitors on safety.

· Dolerite – a hard volcanic rock – and chalk were both mined at Larrybane, dolerite in the nineteenth century and chalk from the 1930s to the 1970s. A huge lime kiln stands beside a small café at the edge of the car park. On the Carrick-a-Rede islands, basalt dominates, with ash layers in the north- and west-facing cliffs. Sixty million years ago, this was an explosive volcano, and today seabirds (razorbills, guillemots, kittiwakes and fulmars) nest amongst the shattered and eroded rocks and ash. The fishery dates from the seventeenth century, and Carrick-a-Rede is generally translated as 'the rock in the road' – the 'road' being the east-to-west sea route of migrating Atlantic salmon.

Stop 11: Portaneevey car park. Portaneevey – 'the Port of the Caves' – lies below these cliffs. The viewpoint at the fenced-off cliff-top, approached by a surfaced path, is worth a visit for the outlook to Carrick-a-Rede and the more distant vista of islands, mountains and cliffs, from Fair Head across to Scotland. The view is well interpreted by information panels.

Stop 12: Kinbane Castle. A narrow road leads to a car park. From here, past the tiny, grassy-roofed ice house (which once served the former salmon fishery in the bay below), a path becomes a long set of steep steps descending to a remote cove. At the base of the beautiful, narrow chalk headland of Kinbane sit the remains of another stone castle, built in 1547 by Colla Dubh McDonnell, elder brother of Sorley Boy McDonnell of Dunluce Castle. The castle was still occupied in the mid-eighteenth century, but now all that remains is a gate tower and some flanking walls. These remains are unstable in places and should be treated with care. Just off the headland, the Atlantic swirls and boils on Carrickmannon – the rock of Manann, an Irish sea god, a sort of Celtic Neptune, whose name is also linked with the Isle of Man in the Irish Sea. The dark basalt outcrop of Gobe Feagh – Ravens' Point – towers over the west end of the small bay, with prostrate clumps of juniper clinging to the terraced soil slips on its slopes.

Stop 13: Ballycastle – North Street viewpoint. As you descend the steep hill above the harbour, there is a small viewpoint with an information panel near the cliff-edge. By now, you have left the Causeway Coast Area of Outstanding Natural Beauty and entered the equally beautiful, less rugged landscape of the Glens of Antrim. A daily ferry service operates, weather permitting, from the harbour to Rathlin Island – summer home to about a quarter of a million seabirds, and permanent home to just under a hundred islanders.

APPENDIX 1
Designations

A number of international, national and regional designations of protective and conservation relevance have been declared for Causeway coast sites.

World Heritage Site – Giant's Causeway

The World Heritage Convention seeks to promote international co-operation in the protection of sites which are of exceptional interest and of universal value. In 1986, the Convention added the Giant's Causeway, including seventy-one hectares of adjacent coastline, to its list of sites and monuments. The Causeway meets two of the criteria for an outstanding natural property: it is a prime example of the earth's evolutionary history during the Tertiary epoch; and it contains rare and superlative natural phenomena. The outstanding cultural value of the nearby wreck of the *Girona* is also recognised, as it is a nautical archaeological site associated with an event of international historical significance.

National Nature Reserve – Giant's Causeway

In 1987, the Giant's Causeway, with seventy-one hectares of adjacent coastline, was designated a National Nature Reserve by the Department of the Environment for Northern Ireland. National Nature Reserves are managed specifically to conserve nature and to promote education and research. The Department works closely with the National Trust, which owns and manages the reserve, to ensure that the site is protected and that visitors are given the opportunity to discover and enjoy the geological wonders and wildlife of the Causeway and the surrounding cliffs. Another National Nature Reserve on the Causeway Coast is the Portrush Sill.

Causeway Coast Area of Outstanding Natural Beauty

The north coast of Co Antrim, between Portrush and Ballycastle, including the Giant's Causeway, is one of the most spectacular coastlines in Europe. The Department of the Environment for Northern Ireland designated the Causeway Coast Area of Outstanding Natural Beauty in 1989. This designation formally recognises that the coast and adjacent farmland is a landscape of national importance. The purpose of this designation is to help protect – and, where possible, improve – this landscape, for the benefit of those living in the area and of the many visitors who come to see and enjoy its natural beauty. The Antrim Coast and Glens Area of Outstanding Natural Beauty (including Rathlin Island) is adjacent to the Causeway Coast; it begins just west of Ballycastle town.

Areas of Special Scientific Interest

These are areas deemed to be of scientific interest by reason of their wildlife, their natural vegetation, or their geological, physiographical or other special features. The Department of the Environment for Northern Ireland has designated a number of such areas on the Causeway Coast – for example, Ramore Head and Skerries, Portballintrae, Runkerry, White Park Bay, Sheep Island and Carrick-a-Rede.

APPENDIX 2
Tourist Information

Many organisations, from government departments to local bodies, have roles on the Causeway Coast. The following is a summary of key local contacts. Tourist Information Centres and local authority offices can provide further information.

How to find the Giant's Causeway
The Giant's Causeway is situated on the north coast of Co Antrim, 3km north of the town of Bushmills. The Causeway's Irish Grid reference is C946447.
A useful map is the Ordnance Survey of Northern Ireland 1:50,000, scale sheet 5 (Ballycastle) of the *Discoverer* series.

Access is from the B146 road, off the A2. Cyclists can follow the NCN Route 93. For public transport, use Ulsterbus service 172 from Portrush to Ballycastle, or their Antrim Coaster service 252 from Belfast. The nearest Northern Ireland Railways stations are at Portrush and Coleraine.

The Causeway itself is always open to pedestrians, and the Visitor Centre and other tourist facilities at the site are open regularly (see below).

Giant's Causeway Visitor Centre
44 Causeway Road
Bushmills
Co Antrim
BT57 8SU
Tel: (028) 2073-1855
Note: Most of the Visitor Centre at the Giant's Causeway was destroyed by fire on 30 April 2000. The owners, Moyle District Council, are to erect temporary tourist reception and retailing facilities as soon as possible, and are consulting with the National Trust and other partners to plan rebuilding of the Centre. The Giant's Causeway itself was not affected.

Tourist Information Centres are located in Ballycastle, Portrush and Coleraine, and at the Giant's Causeway Visitor Centre. All provide information and accommodation listings, and sell leaflets and maps. Further information is available from the local authorities:

Moyle District Council
Sheskburn House
7 Mary Street
Ballycastle
Co Antrim
Tel: (028) 2076-2024

Coleraine Borough Council
Cloonavin
41 Portstewart Road
Coleraine
Co Londonderry
Tel: (028) 7035-2181

Environmental contacts

Environment and Heritage Service
Department of the Environment for Northern Ireland
Portrush Countryside Centre
Bath Terrace
Portrush
Co Antrim
Tel: (028) 7082-3600

The National Trust
North Coast Office
60 Causeway Road
Bushmills
Co Antrim
BT57 8SU
Tel: (028) 2073-1582

In case of emergency, the Coastguard can be reached by dialling 999. There are Coastguard stations at Ballycastle and Portrush.

The author and publisher thank the following for permission to use photographs and illustrative material: Ulster Museum, colour section 1, pp.6 and 7 (top) 'East Prospect of the Giant's Causeway (1739)' by Susanna Drury, *fl.* 1733–1770, colour section 2, *Girona* treasure, p.8; Welch print, 'Naturalists at the Causeway 1868', pp.26 and 27, Welch print, 'In the Wishing Chair, Giant's Causeway', p.46, Welch print 244, 'Giant's Well', reproduced with the kind permission of the trustees of the National Museums and Galleries of Northern Ireland, p.51; National Trust, pp.13, 16, 30, 63, 65, colour section 1, p.2 (top), p.5 (bottom); Environment and Heritage Service, pp. 1, 8, 19, 23, 28, 29, 70, 71, 72, 74, 81, 86, 88, colour section 1, p.1, p.2 (bottom), p.3 (both), p.4 (both), p.5 (both), p.7 (bottom), p.8, colour section 2, p.1 (bottom), p.2 (bottom), p.3 (both), p.4 (both), p.6 (bottom) p.7; J. Taylor, p.10, colour section 2, p.5; D. Speers, p.33; Ulster Folk and Transport Museum, W.A. Green Collection 263, 'Kelp Burning', p.36, reproduced with the kind permission of the trustees of the National Museums and Galleries of Northern Ireland; the late Miss Peg Pollock, p.38 (both), p.47; Tom McDonald, p.34; Robert Anderson, p.66; Author's own pictures, pp.14, 18, 34 (bottom), 39, 40, 67, 69, 76, 77, colour section 2, p.2 (top), p.6 (top); Author's collection, pp.11, 12, 20, 37, 44, 49, 53, 54, 58, 59, 84, colour section 2, p.1 (top). Front cover photograph: 'The Causeway stones', Environment and Heritage Service. Back cover photographs: 'Where myth meets science: Finn MacCool and the Causeway stones', McCann Erickson, Belfast, Ltd.; the author by the Giant's Boot in 1985, National Trust.

BIBLIOGRAPHY

Many sources were used as references in the writing of this book. The following is a selection of popular works still in print. Useful local sources include *The Bann Disc* (Journal of the Coleraine Historical Association), *The Glynns* (Journal of the Glens of Antrim Historical Society), and *Portcaman* (Occasional Publication of the Bushmills Folklore and History Group).

Barne, J.H. et al., 1997. *Coasts and Seas of the United Kingdom. Region 17, Northern Ireland.* Peterborough, Joint Nature Conservation Committee (Coastal Directories Series).

Brett, C.E.B. and M. O'Connell, 1996. *Buildings of County Antrim.* Ulster Architectural Heritage Society and the Ulster Historical Foundation, Belfast.

Carter, R.W.G., 1991. *Shifting Sands: A Study of the Coast of Northern Ireland from Magilligan to Larne.* HMSO, Belfast.

Cecil, T., 1990. *The Harsh Winds of Rathlin: Stories of Rathlin Shipwrecks.* Impact Printing, Coleraine.

Dallat, C., 1990. *Antrim Coast and Glens: A Personal View.* HMSO, Belfast.

Dallat, C., 1990. *A Tour of the Causeway Coast.* Friar's Bush Press, Belfast.

Department of the Environment for Northern Ireland (undated). *Causeway Coast Area of Outstanding Natural Beauty* (leaflet). Environment and Heritage Service, DoENI.

Department of the Environment for Northern Ireland, 1989. *Causeway Coast Area of Outstanding Natural Beauty: Guide to Designation.* DoENI.

Gallagher, L. and D. Rogers, 1992. *Castle, Coast and Cottage: The National Trust in Northern Ireland.* The Blackstaff Press (second edition), Belfast.

Glens of Antrim Historical Society, 1988. *M'Cahan's Local Histories: A Series of Pamphlets On North Antrim And The Glens (1923)*. Compiled by Cahal Dallat. Glens of Antrim Historical Society.

Hammond, F., 1991. *Industrial Heritage – Antrim Coast and Glens*. HMSO, Belfast.

Lyle, P., 1996. *A Geological Excursion Guide to the Causeway Coast*. Environment and Heritage Service, DoENI.

McGuigan, J.H., 1983. *Giant's Causeway, Portrush and Bush Valley Railway and Tramway Co. Ltd*. Ulster Folk and Transport Museum.

Marshall, J., 1991. *Forgotten Places of the North Coast*. Clegnagh Publishing, Mosside, Co Antrim.

Marshall, J., 1998. *Dalriada: A Guide around the Celtic Kingdom*. Glenariff Development Group, Co Antrim.

National Trust, 1997. *Education: The Giant's Causeway – A Resource Book for Teachers*. The National Trust (Education), Northern Ireland.

Polin, D., 1999. *The Drontheim: Forgotten Sailing Boat of the North Irish Coast*. PlayPrint Ltd. (2nd edition), Dublin.

Wilson, I., 1997. *Shipwrecks of the Ulster Coast*. Impact Printing Ltd. (third edition), Coleraine.